THE SHE BOOK OF CATS

The SHE book of CATS

by
Pamela Carmichael

BOOK CLUB ASSOCIATES
LONDON

This edition published 1984 by
Book Club Associates
by arrangement with Ebury Press
National Magazine House,
72 Broadwick Street,
London W1V 2BP.

Design by Bob Hall.

Artist Paula Youens.

Filmset in Great Britain by
Advanced Filmsetters (Glasgow) Ltd.

**Printed in Great Britain at the
University Press, Cambridge**

Photographic credits: *page 2* Marc Henri;
8 Spectrum; *9* Marc Henri: *10* (top)
Bruce Coleman, (bottom) Spectrum; *11*
Richard & Sally Greenhill; *12* (left)
Spectrum, (right) Kate Lockley; *13*
Keystone; *14* British Museum; *15* Mansell;
16 British Museum; *17* British Museum;
18 British Museum; *19* Mansell; *21* John
Topham; *22* Mansell; *23* John Topham;
24 Panther Photographic; *25* Panther
Photographic; *26* Panther Photographic;
27 Marc Henri; *29* Marc Henri; *31* Marc
Henri; *32* Marc Henri; *37* Marc Henri; *38*
Sally Anne Thompson; *39* Panther
Photographic; *40* Panther Photographic;
43 Marc Henri; *44* Panther Photographic;
45 Marc Henri; *46* Panther Photographic;
47 Sally Anne Thompson; *48* Spectrum;
49 Marc Henri; *50* Marc Henri; *51* Panther
Photographic; *53* Panther Photographic;
55 Panther Photographic; *56* Panther
Photographic; *57* Panther Photographic; *58*
Vision International; *59* Marc Henri; *60* Sally
Anne Thompson; *61* Spectrum; *63* Marc
Henri; *64* Panther Photographic; *65* Rex
Features; *67* John Topham; *68* John
Topham; *69* Spectrum; *70* Spectrum; *72*
Kate Lockley; *73* Spectrum; *74* Marc Henri;
75 Panther Photographic; *76/77* Panther
Photographic; *78* Panther Photographic; *79*
Spectrum; *81* Marc Henri; *82* Marc Henri;
83 John Topham; *84* Marc Henri; *85* Marc
Henri; *86/87* John Topham; *89* Panther
Photographic; *90* Spectrum; *91* Mansell; *92*
John Topham; *95* Mansell; *96/97* John
Topham; *98* Mansell; *99* Mansell; *100* Paul
Tanqueray; *103* John Topham; *104* Panther
Photographic; *105* Richard & Sally
Greenhill; *107* Sally Anne Thompson

Front cover: Lucy Su
Back cover: Karen Norquay

Contents

O Cats

O Cats.

You who condescend to inhabit our homes, to accept our offerings of food and shelter and affection, yet reserve always the right to be in control of your own destiny.

You who still walk alone.

O cats, you are beautiful in all your moods (and well you know it!). When you permit us to stroke you, your fur is soft and delightful. When you purr, your voice is kind and comforting.

O cats, it is good to have you around.

May you perhaps learn to be a little less cruel, allowing the mice from which you keep our houses free to die a quicker death (let's have less tossing in the air, patting from paw to paw, teasing with brief escapes, before the final pounce). May you spare the birds, especially fledglings. And the butterflies.

May you make less noise at night, when courting or quarrelling on our garden walls.

May you forswear destruction indoors, performing your claw-sharpening routines not on carpets and furniture but outside on trees, posts and fences.

May you occasionally give up the best chair with a good grace, when a human who lives with you wishes to sit on it. And could you please refrain from hogging the *middle* of the bed every night.

May you even, once in a while, jump on to someone's lap and remain there — with no ulterior motive, mind you — for at least as long as it takes to untangle a cat's cradle.

But O cats, both purrfect and impurrfect, whatever you get up to — you are really very welcome.

Please stay.

Pamela Carmichael

The Nature of Cats

Cats have the collective reputation of being aloof, lacking in affection, undemonstrative and overly independent. But most people who think and say such things about cats are not cat owners. Indeed they have probably been rejected or abandoned by cats at one time or another because of their own off-hand behaviour, so they are unlikely to be cat lovers or even cat likers. They certainly do not *understand* cats. Everyone who loves cats and lives with cats, who takes the trouble to get to know them properly, will tell you that the very opposite is true. As a race domestic cats are friendly, affectionate, deeply dependent on their humans for love, care and security. Why the apparent contradiction?

It's simple, really. Cats, like people, have to learn to trust. Cats, like people, have their pride. So no cat ever fawns on strangers in the hope of being well treated. He prefers to keep his distance to begin with, and see what's what and who's who. That's not being aloof, just reasonably cautious. Furthermore he's not going to risk a rebuff: he'd rather sit quietly and mind his own business until he's called forward—and *that's* when he'll come if he wants and not if he doesn't, accord-

ing to the opinion of you he's so far arrived at. Can you blame him?

If a person shows tact, by not fussing the cat, picking him up and interrupting his train of thought; if a person shows warmth and understanding, and has the wit to provide security and food without looking for immediate reward in the shape

of purrs and rubbings against legs, and if the person is consistent in this enlightened attitude, then that could be the beginning of friendship.

However, without being too sexist, it does seem that women have an advantage where cats are concerned. On the whole, cats trust women more readily than they trust men. And for that the only explanation I can put forward (other than the cynical one that it's more often than not the woman of the house who opens the tins or cooks the cat's food, puts it on his plate and calls him to breakfast or supper) is the one in Rudyard Kipling's Just-So Story, *The Cat That Walked By Himself*.

Remember? The Wild Cat was told by the Woman that because he had not come with the Wild Dog when she made magic with roast mutton—so that Wild Dog promised never to be wild again and became First Friend—Wild Cat could never come into the cave, never drink warm white milk from the cow, never sit beside the warm hearth. But Wild Cat made a bargain with the Woman that if ever she said three words in his praise, he would after all be allowed all three of these privileges—yet he would still remain the Cat That Walked

By Himself. In due course Woman did praise the Wild Cat; because he helped look after her baby, he made it laugh, and he killed a mouse which frightened her. So he came into the cave, and drank the milk, and sat by the fire. But when the Man and the First Friend (ex-Wild Dog) came home from hunting, they paid no attention to the bargain he'd made with the Woman, and chased him away. And ever since then the Man and the Dog have been the Cat's enemies, and Woman has been his friend.

Just as the personalities of men and women depend partly on heredity and partly on upbringing, a cat's nature is governed in part by his breed. We'll go into pedigree breeds in more detail in another chapter. But as a quick example it's well known now—because they're so popular and widely owned—that Siamese cats are super-intelligent, constantly in communication with anyone who'll listen, and totally demanding; they take over their owners' lives and refuse to be neglected for a moment. In self-defence, the best thing to do is to own two of them: they may gang up against you from time to time but by giving them the companionship of their own species you stand a chance of taking some of the emotional heat out of your own relationship with your pet(s).

I don't know about the personalities of other high grade eastern and Middle-Eastern breeds from experience, but research indicates that the Havana Brown, Burmese and Bombay need company more

Cats are hunters, seekers, finders; equally at home relaxing on the hearth or plotting mischief up a tree . . .

9

Now just do as I tell you—or else!

than most others (so will probably complain if left alone for long); and the Abyssinian not only dislikes being left alone but can't *bear* any sort of confinement. It would probably cause mayhem if taken to live in a small flat or even a garden-less house. The well-known British Shorthair (you meet him every-where) is as sturdy in mind as he is in body and self-reliant to the point of cunning; he gets deeply attached to places as well as to people, and by about one year of age knows his own patch as well as the back of his paws; furthermore he'll fight anyone who attempts to intrude upon it.

Otherwise most cats—once they've settled down into good homes where they are well cared for—really *are* friendly, well-disposed to one-and-all (including children and babies), gentle and quiet.

Cats do not like moving house and they will go to considerable lengths to avoid doing so. There have been stories of cats, transported against their will to a new home miles away, walking determinedly

back to the old one. If you must move, do tell your cat about it well in advance (like weeks ahead) and tell him again repeatedly so that he realises you *mean* it. As the moving day draws near, let him help you pack—I mean you should encourage him to sit and watch while you get on with it. (This psychological preparation also helps if you are leaving your cat[s] at home while you go away on holiday. Pack your suitcase a day ahead of time and let him/them sleep on it—it seems to calm apprehension remarkably.) If he won't take an interest, or even worse, runs away and hides, this is a warning that there's going to be trouble. Find out where he's disappearing to, by all means, but don't let him know you know or he'll find another refuge and you won't know where to look for him at the last minute. If he's more phlegmatic, spots a box he fancies and goes to sleep in it, thank your lucky stars and christen it his very own moving box. Encourage him to spend as much time as he likes in it, put him into it on the day of the move and, if it can be made secure, let him travel in it. If not get it out ready for him the moment you arrive at the new place—yes, even before you make a cuppa for the moving men.

A cat which is disturbed by a move can behave in a really crazy fashion. I know—we've had one! Take heart, she's purrfectly all right now. But at the time the whole household was just about as upset as she was; we were at our wits' end and so was she. Until we found and blocked off the tiny hole through which she got into it, she spent hours in the roof space, howling and frightening herself even more as her voice echoed around her in the emptiness.

After we'd sealed the hole into the roof she made do with an attic windowsill, on which she sat all day and looked out mournfully at the new landscape. She refused all offers of food but at least she came down one flight of stairs to use the litter tray—which for the time being we put in our bathroom—and we comforted ourselves with this small sign that she wasn't completely off her head. But she wouldn't let us touch her, wouldn't talk to us, wouldn't do anything but hate the place. Oh yes, she did, by the way, rip up the new stair carpet if she thought we weren't anywhere about (I know she had to exercise her shoulder muscles and keep her claws down somehow, but who wants a poodle-effect stair carpet?). At first we tried coaxing, then just leaving her alone. After a few days we were worried enough to bring her downstairs against her will and put titbits of her most favourite food in front of her. But she never ate any, just paced around the kitchen yelling, and escaped upstairs as soon as she could.

Eventually we lost patience and said 'Oh, starve if you want to then!' And that seemed to be the

beginning of her recovery, that and the Christmas holidays when the house was full of people and there was less time available to spend trying to coax her. As we relaxed, so did she. Gradually she appeared downstairs more often, though she (who formerly had nerves of steel) was always liable to hide again at the slightest unexpected noise, or if a stranger entered the room.

She'd lost weight, but she'd always been a healthy cat and she started eating again, albeit a little capriciously. In a week or two she looked almost her old self. She even ventured outdoors. By the end of the first three months the house was hers and the garden thereof too. If asked, she'd probably have forgotten what all fuss was about.

But come to think of it how would you and I feel if we were suddenly put in a car and driven miles to a new home, leaving behind a house and garden that was familiar, dear and safe? No wonder she made a fuss. And yet her daughter, going through exactly the same experience, didn't appear to suffer at all: she travelled placidly, inspected our/ her new domain and checked that all her favourite furniture (*e.g.* big easy chair, sofa, nice soft beds) was somewhere about, and settled down at once. There's no accounting for temperament, obviously— unless you decide that the cat which most hates moving must be more attached to a place, her old home, while the other puts her people first and says, with Ruth in the Bible, 'Whither thou goest, I will go.'

Cats are like people, in fact. Treat them right and they'll usually be quite good to you in return. Don't,

Left: Oh I do love you really . . .
Right: How strange, running around the garden with no fur on!

and they won't either. Very few cats are born all mean: I once knew a family who acquired two cross-eyed Siamese brothers which deliberately, I swear it was deliberate, destroyed the top of a grand piano by using it as a scratching surface/post. In spite of pepper and other deterrents they persisted, and their besotted owners refused either to move the piano or to forbid the cats to enter the music room. But even those two managed to be endearing when not engaged in destruction, and so escaped the come-uppance which I felt they so richly deserved.

Young cats can be very destructive, but in most cases that can be stopped or at least the damage mitigated by providing substitute playthings. They can also scratch

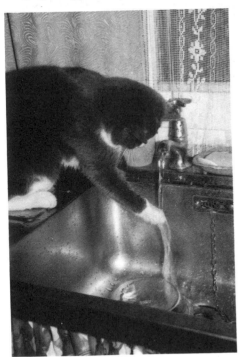

Testing the water. Now if Boots would only do the dishes too!

people—mostly by mistake—but one expert believes that unless a young cat is taught never to scratch in play he can cause a lot of trouble when he is older. She therefore recommends owners never to use their hands as a 'plaything' for the kitten—hands are for stroking or for picking up. For a plaything—which can be caught in sharp, extended claws—offer a toy mouse, a twist of paper, a length of string.

Cats can be either difficult in illness or remarkably brave, just as humans can. We've experienced both. One went just about berserk at the idea of allowing the vet to give her a routine injection. Another of the same family suffered the most horrible attack of a skin disease—which itched her, hurt and disfigured her, removed most of her fur and gummed up her eyes—not only without complaint, but without once flinching during essential but painful treatment. She recovered, I'm glad to say, and her coat is once more beautiful. We know now that her even temperament conceals a spirit incredibly brave and enduring.

What else about the nature of cats? Well most cats can be pretty mischievous, I suppose, but this rarely lasts after the first year except as an occasional flashback. Some cats are rasher than others—these are the ones which manage to climb to the top of the tree and then need the fire brigade to bring them down safely—but again this is a rare occurrence beyond kittenhood.

Cats are quite capable of being sulky. Ours don't like us leaving home, even for a day; if we go on holiday we always make arrangements for them to stay in their own home with well-known and much-loved cat-minders in charge, but that doesn't really please them either.

There's a lot to be said for not taking sides . . .

On one occasion when we'd been in France for two weeks we arrived home longing to see them and ask them how they'd been; they were sitting on a table as we entered the room, watching the door, but as we crossed towards them they simultaneously rose, turned as one cat and sat down again with their backs to us. We stopped in our tracks, our Hellos wilting in our throats. It wasn't, we knew in our hearts, that they weren't pleased to see us; but they had disapproved of our absence and now we knew that they had, because they'd shown us. They sulked silently for a day or two and then they forgot about it; all was forgiven.

Cats can also be jealous, both of humans and of each other. Stroke one, stroke all, is a wise rule. Feed one with a titbit, find something equally delicious for the others, or

The scavenging instinct is still alive in a world where there are poor cats as well as rich ones. This little moggie was quick to spot a free dinner

woe will betide. Never offer a visiting cat the basket of someone already living in the house or there will be trouble.

Every cat is an individual, that's worth remembering. Just as you are, and I am. They all have their little ways. One cat is moderate and another greedy, one slow and one fast, one interested and one self-absorbed. I think that possibly the worst insult you can offer cats is to treat them all alike, call them in conversation 'the cats' instead of Tiddles and Alexander, or Mary and Boo. Do you think your cats call you 'the people' when they discuss you behind your back?

I've known wise cats and stupid cats, sly cats and honest cats; we've had a female cat which adored producing kittens and one young mother which hated the whole process and became seriously ill afterwards (could the complaint have been psychosomatic?). We've known brave tomcats and terrified ones. We will never forget a timid spirit (which looked huge but really couldn't stand violence) being chased from end to end of a passage upstairs in the dead of night by a marauding marmalade swashbuckler which had decided to steal in through a back bedroom window in search of female talent. Far from protecting his wife and daughters, our hero was in sad need of pro-

tection himself. His screams and those of his attacker woke us up.

There are also naturally comical cats and deliberately serious cats, silly cats like the poet Thomas Grey's, which drowned in a goldfish pond, and seductive cats like the beauty which inspired Edward Lear's sea-going owl to sing to her so romantically.

All cats, in fact have character. All cats are worth getting to know.

First Cats

Where did cats come from in the first place? Since they made their original appearance among humans many thousands of years ago, and no one among those now present was around to record the event, it's impossible to say for certain. But experts seem to agree that domestic cats as we now know them evolved from the African Wildcat (*Felis libyca*) and the European Wildcat (*Felis sylvestris*). Briefly tracing their ancestry even farther back in time, fifty million years ago there lived creatures called *Miacids* — long-bodied, short-legged and carnivorous. Ten million years later, one branch of their descendants, the *Dinictis*, looked rather like lynxes except that they had exceptionally large canine teeth. From *Dinictis* seem to have evolved not only the now-extinct sabre-toothed tiger of ancient times but also the *Felidae* family to which all today's cats belong: not just domestic cats, mind you, but wild and feral ones, as well as lions, tigers, lynxes, cheetahs, and pumas. So the innocently purring moggie on the hearth beside you has some truly fearsome close relations!

It seems probable that the wild cats of times gone by, hunting small animals like rats and mice for their food, discovered that although these could be come upon singly or in small groups in open countryside, they existed in far greater numbers around places where human beings made their homes. Rats were scavengers, feeding on discarded food; both mice and rats were thieves, stealing the grain which men and women worked so hard to plant and to harvest and which was such an important part of their diet.

Sometime, somewhere — possibly in a settlement on the banks of the Euphrates or the Nile — it must have started to dawn on people that cats were useful to have around. Cats didn't pick over rubbish tips for food, they were much too choosy, they preferred to catch their own food — alive — kill it and then eat it hot and raw. Cats were straightforward, bloody minded carnivores so it never occurred to them to steal grain. Where cats appeared, the plaguey rats and mice seemed to disappear. So in no time — probably only a thousand years or two

Left: This Egyptian bronze cat, collared with the eye of Horus, was probably made after the cult of Bast had died out. But affection for the cat had come to stay.
Right: Adam and Eve, the world's first man and wife, come complete with a cat at their feet in this engraving by Dürer

14

—cats became well accepted. No doubt at the beginning they were wary and stayed out of reach because humans were so unpredictable; but gradually they learned to come indoors occasionally and settle down beside a warm hearth.

Earliest known records of cats were made by the Egyptians, which strengthens the theory about them becoming acceptable due to their rat/mouse catching talents, because in those days Egypt grew vast acreages of grain in the Nile valley and acquired enormous wealth therefrom. Cats became, in fact, vital to the Egyptian economy and gradually they acquired great symbolic importance. For example the Sun God, Ra, was believed to assume the form of a cat every day at dawn in order to drive away the night by killing Apep, the serpent of darkness. There's a representation of the actual happening on a 3,200-year-old scroll of the Book of the Dead, though somewhat oddly Ra is beheading Apep with a knife whereas any rightminded cat would surely have done it with his own sharp teeth and claws!

Another deity, this time the goddess Bastet, still exists in statue form as a woman with a cat's head and a couple of alert and charming kittens at her feet. Bastet's more usual name was Bast, and she was worshipped at Bubastis on the lower Nile, so records say, from at least 1780 BC until about 392 AD—quite a span of time for any god or goddess. Her temple cats are said to have had special guardians, whose duty it was to watch them constantly for any sign of a communication from the goddess. If a worshipper hoped for some special favour he had to shave the head of one of his children, take the hair to the temple and have it weighed, then present an equal weight of silver to the guardians and with it they would buy fish for the sacred cats! After a good meal the cats would no doubt feel more like intervening on the supplicant's behalf.

One shouldn't forget of course that the Egyptians were in the habit of making quite a lot of fuss over other animals and reptiles—snakes, lions, monkeys, hawks all feature in their religion, as almost every god or goddess had an animal of his/her own—but cats do seem to have been pre-eminent.

Gradually families began keeping

A smiling, seated Bast (pronounced 'Pasht', from which the word 'Puss' is said to derive) waits at the British Museum for offerings which never come

cats as domestic pets, greatly loved and even revered. When their cat died the whole household went into mourning, some people even shaving off their eyebrows as an extreme sign of their grief. Cats were mummified after death: early excavations at Bubastis revealed hundreds of them, embalmed and entombed, so it's thought possible that not only the sacred temple cats were buried there but also those of devotees.

When a cat was buried in a private tomb it was often honoured with a bronze or even gold casket, and beside its mummified body was left food—mummified mice, of course—plus carvings of sacred cats to guard it and make its journey to the world of the dead as easy as possible.

Anyone who injured a cat in the Egypt of those days was subject to severe penalties, and it was absolutely forbidden to export cats—some say because by this time the Egyptians thought the animals had the power to protect them from evil. People even wore jewellery made in the image of cats, as good luck charms. (Have you ever been given a 'lucky black cat' greetings card, or found one as a charm in a cracker perhaps? It's a long time for a superstition to last, isn't it?)

One wall painting from a tomb in Thebes shows a delicious marmalade-coloured cat surrounded by wildfowl of all sorts, also butterflies and flowers. Maybe he was just part of the design, put in as one of the many creatures his master loved to have around him during his lifetime—but as the said master is also in the painting some experts inter-

In this wall painting in Thebes, a cat accompanies his master—as a retriever in a wildfowl hunt?—as a tame visitor in an aviary? We will probably never know

(8) MUMMIED CAT [37348]

pret it as proof that Egyptians even trained their cats as retrievers.

It's thought that most Egyptian cats were originally small African wildcats, *Felis libyca.* And gradually, in spite of the laws forbidding export, they started to turn up in India and China too, probably via Greece and the Middle East where Phoenician traders brought them by sea. There's a story that the Chinese believed they could tell the time of day by looking into a cat's eyes: if the pupils were tiny it was morning or early afternoon, in the evening and at night they were much larger. Which seems a bit obvious to us because we know now that a cat's pupils do grow huge in the dark, to let in the maximum amount of light, and they get correspondingly tiny when there is plenty of light about—but it was an original idea in those days.

Probably those Phoenician traders who took cats aboard did so in the hope of keeping down the rats which traditionally live on ships and pilfer scarce food; possibly they took them along because they were a novelty and might appeal to some rich trader in foreign parts; maybe they just liked having cats for company; maybe the cats insisted, fancying a change of scene. Anyhow they certainly managed to spread them around, and by the time the Roman Empire was established, cats were popular in Italy and southern France, chiefly because they kept down vermin but also because they made companionable domestic pets.

It's thought that the Romans, as well as those ubiquitous Phoenician traders, may have introduced cats into Britain, though by that time the European Wildcat, *Felis sylvestris,* is surely likely to have made contact with human settlements and started to perform the same services

for people in northern Europe as its cousins in Egypt had been doing for centuries. Certainly it didn't take long for cats to colonise the British Isles, and by the ninth century AD they were well established and highly valued. Anyone deliberately harming or killing a cat was liable to be fined, and if a cat was a proven mouser—even if it had so far killed only one mouse—it was worth at least two pence, a worthwhile sum of money in those days.

Unhappily for cats, all this hardearned and well-deserved popularity didn't last. It's not quite clear how the transformation came about, but by the Middle Ages cats had acquired a sinister reputation which terrified some people and spurred others to acts of great cruelty. Cats were said to be agents of the devil, foul spirits, witches . . . And witches were thought to be able to turn into cats. Two possible influences may have worked on superstitious minds. First, there was a pagan goddess called Freya who was said to have had her chariot drawn by two black cats; second, the Romans had linked the Egyptian cat goddess, Bast, with their Artemis, or Diana, goddess of the moon, who in turn was thought to be close to or even the same person as Hecate, goddess of witches. These ladies were strictly anti-Christian at a time when the Church's influence was strong.

Whatever caused it, Europe was seized by a wave of cat fear and cat hatred, particularly on the part of the Church, which should surely have known better. Many people believed, or thought they did, that the Devil was wont to appear on earth as a black cat, and after one terrible night in 1344 when such an appearance was blamed for an outbreak of St. Vitus' Dance (a kind of mass hysteria, very likely) in the

Left: Mummified cats are common finds in Egyptian tombs. Above: Folklore sees black cats as familiars of witches, the 'Grimalkin' of legend in both Britain and Germany

town of Metz, thirteen cats were publicly burned alive. Burnings took place in other cities, and at one place cats were hurled from a church belfry to their death. Pope Innocent VII, at the end of the 15th century, instructed the agents of the Inquisition to seek out 'cat-worshippers'.

Some cats were hung, others drowned—often with their owners, suspected of being witches. In England persecution reached a peak in the reign of Elizabeth I when an effigy of the current Pope was carried through the streets of London with caged live cats inside it; the effigy was eventually burned, and the screams of the tortured cats were said (triumphantly!) to be those

of Catholic devils. After Elizabeth's death King James I carried on the hunt for witches, and it was not really safe for anyone to own a cat unless it was clearly kept outdoors, earning its keep as a mouser and definitely not a friend of the family or a 'familiar'. If you were female, single, solitary, the slightest bit unconventional, or elderly, it was much much safer to get yourself a good big dog (preferably fierce).

It wasn't all no-go for cats everywhere, fortunately. Quite a lot of people continued to value them (even if secretly) for their mouse-catching skills; others, in still greater secrecy, continued to enjoy their company as pets. In one area in southern France people believed in lucky cats, *matapots*, which had the power to bring good fortune to homes in which they were kindly and hospitably received. A retired sixth-century Pope had a cat as his only companion, so did an Irish

monk; another Pope allowed a much-loved cat to sit on his knee, albeit hidden in the folds of his robes, while he gave audiences, and Cardinal Wolsey had a cat which he took to church. Cardinal Richelieu is said to have owned fourteen cats at one time.

As inexplicably as the persecution had begun, gradually it died down. Cats became acceptable again, and taken more or less for granted. Being philosophical, or perhaps just fruitful, they bore no grudges, settled back into their old ways, and multiplied. There are now said to be between four and six million of them in the British Isles alone.

But have they ever forgotten? Deep in the tribal memory of every cat, I'm sure, are faint recollections of man's inhumanity, man's foolish superstitions, man's cruelty. Which is why few cats are willing to trust a strange human, on first acquaintance. Well, would you?

Wildcats

It's reasonable to suppose that the European Wildcats (*Felis sylvestris* or 'cat of the trees/woods') must be the far distant descendants of felines which decided, thousands of years ago, that they didn't want to have anything at all to do with humans. Some of their friends and relations settled for the cushy life and eventually became domestic cats, but not them—and it's *their* descendants which still survive in the highlands of Scotland, the forests of France and remote parts of other European countries.

I've seen two wildcats in my life, both of them in France. The sightings were so unexpected, and lasted for so short a time, that it's difficult to be sure of describing them accurately, but the overall impression in both cases was of an exceptionally large and fit tabby cat.

The first one crossed a deserted minor road in a part of Burgundy where the plains are high and forests thick, coming from a meadow on the left to the shelter of trees on the right. It was moving quickly, that's for sure, but not rushing. The time was late afternoon in spring, so dusk would soon be falling but it was still daylight. And in its mouth the cat had a rabbit. It was this that amazed us, brought us up short, made us realise exactly what we'd just seen.

'Did you see it?' asked my husband, stopping the car. 'Did you see what that animal was carrying?'

'The cat, you mean?'

'The wildcat,' he said. 'It must have been. Think where we are—miles from any village, any house. And it was huge, too. It couldn't have been an ordinary cat.'

'Not one *gone* wild?'

'Not that size! Did you *see* it? It had the rabbit by the back and was carrying it clear of the ground; even if it wasn't a very big rabbit that still makes the cat quite a size. It was a wildcat all right!'

We sat in silence for a minute or two, trying to remember just what it had looked like. And the image remained of this very big tabby, strong, lithe and fit, carrying this dead rabbit . . .

The second was a much closer encounter, for me at least. We were walking in a forest in the Jura, quite high in the mountains and quite deep in the forest, following a track which was said to lead to a ruined castle where a medieval queen had once been imprisoned. I'd gone on ahead for some reason, and was rather regretting it. The forest was spooky—maybe filled with ghosts. The trees were tall, the undergrowth thick; small creatures out of sight made scuffling sounds, birds flew from branch to branch but didn't often call, the light of day was diffused by leaves and branches, every now and then a breath of wind sighed through it all. If I see a fallen log, I thought, I'll sit on it and wait until he catches up (he'd been lingering to take photographs, as usual). But no log appeared so I kept on. And because I was walking slowly, I suppose I was fairly silent—which is presumably why, on rounding the next bend in the track, I found myself face to face with this *huge* cat. He/she was bigger than the biggest doctored domestic tabby I've ever seen. He was so amazed to see me that he hadn't time to look fierce—just utterly astonished, with big furry ears still pricked, great golden eyes staring head-on into mine. And I had just enough time to think: He's a wildcat. It must be a wildcat. Oh it's . . . And he'd

Right: This European wildcat may look like a sample of the taxidermist's art—but it isn't. The glassy-eyed glare was provoked by the photographer who snapped it on arrival at London Zoo

gone! Like an owl, which one moment you see and the next it disappears off the branch it was perching on without making a sound, although you know it must have lifted its wings before it floated out of sight. He'd melted silently into the forest, gone without a sound or a trace, not even a quiver of grass or small bushes left to indicate his path. I sat down then on the grass, thinking: Oh I wish I'd had the camera, Oh why did it have to run away so quickly, Oh I wish . . .

'And a very good thing, too,' said Michael, when he caught up. 'Knowing you, a second or two longer and you'd have been trying to make friends, wouldn't you? And that wouldn't have been much fun. It's a long way back to the car and the First Aid kit!'

You don't have to go abroad to see a wildcat. It's possible that you might encounter one in the highlands of Scotland if you were very lucky, very patient, very quiet. But failing such a sighting in its natural habitat you just have to fall back on natural history museums, books, photographs, drawings, because very few wildcats exist in captivity.

What, if any, are the differences between the wildcat and domestic cats? First things first, just in case you do ever meet one in the flesh. Wildcats are definitely *not* friendly towards human beings. Whereas most domestic cats—and even feral cats, which are domestic cats which have 'gone wild' and are looking after themselves due to circumstances beyond their control such as the death of their owner, a household move with which they didn't wish to be associated, abandonment by hard-up or hard-hearted people —can be tempted and in time caught if you try hard enough, a wildcat will run away if encoun-

tered, and if cornered may attack. So the golden rule in the event of a meeting is to leave him alone!

This course of action would probably come naturally, anyhow, as a result of his behaviour. If cornered, or if he thought he was cornered, he'd almost certainly bare his teeth, snarl and spit; his golden eyes would flash, he'd flatten his ears like a domestic tom cat about to go into battle, his tail would be twitching. So should you run? Well unless the wildcat was a female, with kits to defend, it would be unlikely to attack; but discretion is the better part of valour so it might be wise to make yourself scarce—don't panic and rush, just walk away.

However, if the wildcat you've come across has been caught in a trap, which does sometimes occur, please don't just abandon him to his fate—hurry to the nearest post office or police station and report it so that help can be sent.

Apart from behaviour, one of the most noticeable differences between the wildcat and domestic cats is its size. The average length of a wildcat from tip to tail is just under one metre, with a shoulder height of about 37 cm (one giant has been recorded at nearly 1 m 15 cm long!). They have raised hindquarters and extra long hindlegs, too, which give them a distinctive loping action when running.

Another noticeable difference is in the shape and marking of the tail. Domestic cats have plain tails, striped tails; fluffy tails and smooth ones; but nearly all of them are long and taper to a point. The

This print is from a Victorian fauna published in Britain. Weighing between ten and twenty-five pounds, similar cats are still found in mountainous regions all over Europe

wildcat's tail is shorter in proportion to its body and the stripes on it—black, on a paler tabby colour—are wide, distinct, and go round and round instead of up and down. The tail ends in a stumpy black brush, and the fur on it—as on the rest of the body—is thick and almost waterproof. When attacking, or in a pre-attack situation, the wildcat holds its tail straight out behind it, maybe twitching slightly, with the hair fluffed out to make it seem even bigger and thicker. What an alarming sight if you're a rabbit or other small mammal! The tail is also used when swimming, as a kind of rudder—this willingness to get across water barriers such as rivers and lakes is another way in which wildcats differ from domestic ones.

Wildcats are hunters—they have to be. They are exclusively carnivorous. Unlike domestic cats they have no time to play, or can't be bothered with playing, with their prey. When they catch it they kill it and eat it then and there—except when a female is killing for her young, in which case she carries whatever she has been able to find back to the lair and shares it with them. It's thought that wildcats mate only once a year, probably in spring; that a pair remain together for life, although while the female is pregnant and later on feeding her young the male rather ungallantly leaves her to get on with it and doesn't help out in any way. Gestation time is about sixty-three days; the kits are born blind and are helpless within the lair for about four weeks. At about three months

This wildcat was photographed in its natural habitat in Scotland. The relative shortness of the tail and its distinctive marking are particularly apparent in this side view

they go hunting with their mother for the first time; are fully weaned at four months; leave home at six or eight months and are fully-grown at a year old. They now have their full complement of lethal looking teeth, thirty in all: two canines in the upper jaw and two in the lower, twelve incisors, fourteen molars—all the better to crunch their prey with, as their jaws are squarer than the domestic cat's and more powerful.

It's said that a wildcat mother will fight to the death to defend her young, but that no wildcat will ever kill another wildcat—the loser in a fight is always permitted to slink away. (Lacking opportunity for constant observation, the latter is hard to prove.) It's almost certain, and certainly likely, that wildcats mark out their territory just as domestic cats do, spraying or making recognisable marks at various

points to warn other wildcats to keep off. The lair is sometimes in the roots of a tree, but more usually in an inaccessible rocky place.

A point at issue between experts centres on the skull of the European wildcat, which is noticeably flatter than that of the domestic cat and also of the African wildcat from which the first cats in Egypt seem to have descended. Some believe that because wildcats in Europe have this flattened skull, and domestic cats have not, there is no relationship between them. I like to think, as I said at the beginning of this chapter, that *Felis sylvestris* was an obstinate fellow who decided to stay on his wild lone and has done just that, enjoying life on mountains and in forests, keeping his hard, flattish head down and never having anything to do with his comfort-loving cousins. In his opinion, they all went a bit soft!

Choosing Cats

To describe in detail all the many breeds of cat now recognised in the UK, not to speak of the rest of the world, would take a book in itself. And when it was finished it would be superfluous too, because several excellent such books exist already. But to give you some idea of what's available, here followeth a brief run through:

If you seriously wish to own a pedigree cat, your first decision should be whether it's to be a Longhair or a Shorthair. If you think you'd like the former, then someone ought to dissuade you—unless you're absolutely certain that you have the time and patience to cope. Beautiful as long-haired cats may be, loving and equable in temperament, they need regular, daily grooming to keep those superb coats in good condition: are you willing to commit yourself to this? In his introduction to the Standard Guide to Cat Breeds, Consultant Editor Richard H. Gebhardt writes: 'The buyer must be made aware from the beginning of the time and care required to maintain a luxurious coat . . . Too often the novice owner assumes that the animals simply grow up this way.' A Shorthair needs care too, both physical and

emotional, but it doesn't demand anything like as much of the former as a Longhair.

Having made that first decision it's time to go into the matter further. You might, for example, want to own one of the very latest breeds. One breed is so new to show business that it was first awarded a 'Provisional Standard' only in 1979, but so appealing and elegant that it's hard to resist—the Somali, a longish-haired Abyssinian, a fine, handsome cat with medium-long fine hair, dense and double-coated, either ruddy orange-brown in colour, sometimes tipped with black, or warm red, tipped with chocolate. Its eyes are almond-shaped, gold or green. Or you could go for a Classic Longhair (until recently called Persian), fluffy and delicious in a wide range of colours. Like furry ice-creams, they go from pure glistening white through silver-patched tabby to an elegant all-black; they occur in an amazing blue (which looks grey to non-

Left: An award-winning example of a chocolate-point Siamese. Right: Snub-nosed and cuddly, the Blue Persian is a charmer—but don't fall for him unless you're prepared to give his coat regular care

experts) and glorious red–self, which ordinary folk get criticised sometimes for calling marmalade. They may look a bit grumpy because of their short, flat noses (I remember one expert telling me that all Longhairs tend to look cross in repose, but usually aren't anything of the kind, so just to take no notice!) but most of them act kindly towards owners. They do have, however, a proper sense of their own importance and dignity and they do need to be groomed *every* day.

A remarkable man-made breed, comparatively recent, is the Himalayan Colourpoint (Himalayan in the USA) Longhair. This emerged as the result of painstaking cross-breeding between Persians and Siamese: as you'd imagine, it combines the elegant and attractive colouring and points of the Siamese with the Longhair type, and a long and luxurious coat.

The Sacred Cat of Burma—or Birman as it's alternatively known —is said by tradition to have been transformed by a deity from a long-haired white temple cat into a glowing golden one with four white paws and blue eyes. It is very distinctive with its white gloves and Siamese coat pattern, with points which may be seal, blue chocolate or lilac.

The Balinese, with longish white fur, is oriental-looking with a Siamese-shape head, almond-shaped blue eyes, slight but strong body in pale fawn to cream, ivory or white, with no shading at all. The mask, ears, legs, feet and tail may be a deep seal chocolate, blue or lilac.

There is still the Turkish, with

The Burmese combines some of the best qualities of both Siamese and Shorthairs — a firm, elegant body, a sense of humour and a keen intelligence

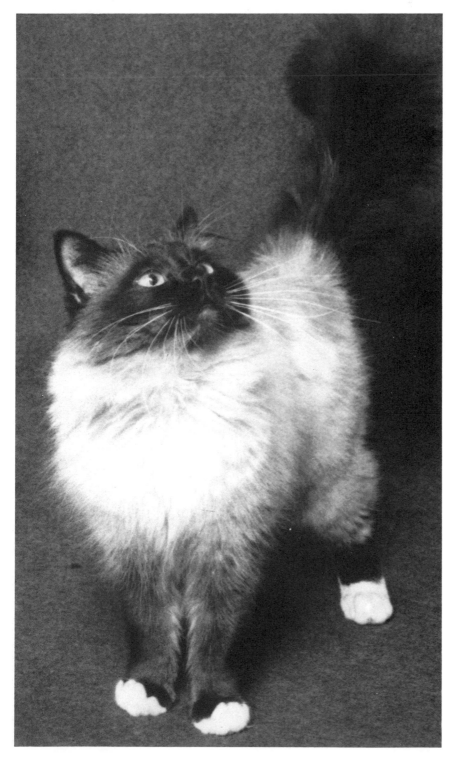

pure white fur, with auburn markings on the face and tail, and the Angora—which may surprise the people who think that all Angoras are rabbits. It looks a bit like a fluffy toy because it's usually pure white, but in the USA it is bred in a number of colours. The toy-like impression is increased when the cats, as does happen, are odd-eyed —one blue and one orange—but they're hardy and charming animals, making good pets.

Now let's turn to the Shorthairs. Among those the best known is still the Siamese, so lean and lithe and handsome, so beautifully pointed, so mischievous, so determined to rule the humans with whom it lives. A Siamese *loves* to talk—in cat language he seems to be continually commenting on everybody and everything—and if he gets annoyed or lonely or frightened he can lift his voice to a pitch not unlike that of a human baby. He has strong emotions: if he loves you he does so vociferously and possessively; if he doesn't, no power on earth will make him come to you. Quite a character, in fact. Make sure you live somewhere where his chatter won't annoy the neighbours.

If you want an exotic and unusual Shorthair you might decide on a Burmese. This has an Oriental look all its own; it's elegant too but more substantial than the Siamese, and always comes in a solid colour with no points (*i.e.* change of colour on head, feet and tail). The most usual colour for the Burmese is deep brown, though cream, blue, chocolate, lilac and tortoiseshell are all recognised. The head is slightly

The Birman—despite the similar-sounding name—is quite different from the Burmese. It's a glamorous Longhair and shows its points and 'socks' early

rounded on top, with wide cheek bones tapering to a blunt wedge, and wide apart yellow eyes; the temperament is even.

Closely related to the Burmese is the Bombay, a fairly new American breed which resulted from crossing Burmese with Black American Shorthairs. This handsome cat has very fine short hair, absolutely black, and golden eyes.

Another rare cat is the Korat, which originated in Thailand. Said to have an especially sweet and loving nature (though apparently in their native land the males are renowned as fighters!), it has a heart-shaped face with large green eyes, large well-pricked ears and fine glossy fur its colour is silver blue.

The beautiful Abyssinian, thought by some experts to be closest of all present day cats to the sacred cats of Egypt, is most usually a rich golden brown colour but it is also bred in copper red, referred to as sorrel, and in a blue-grey colouring. It's quite a long cat, slim but strong, with a wedge-shaped head, large well pricked ears and almond-shaped eyes. It's said to have a gentle, even temperament.

There is the Oriental Spotted Tabby which looks just what its name indicates but which—apart from its looks—has much in common with the Siamese. It is an outgoing, usually friendly but always demanding, personality. In America there is the Egyptian Mau much the same in appearance except that its tabby stripes are more spots than continuous rings. It's claimed to be 'the only natural breed of spotted cat'. And then there is the Havana Brown, developed from the Siamese and therefore resembling it closely in conformation and temperament, but (thank goodness?) said to be not quite so noisy. In fact, this particu-

larly good-looking all-over chestnut brown cat has a gentle nature which matches its usually rather wistful expression.

How many more, you may ask? Well, before coming to the good old British Shorthair, beloved of one and all, we mustn't forget the Russian Blue. One of the earliest breeds shown in the UK around a hundred and thirty years ago, although it is less often seen now. Elegant with its silvery-blue coat, slightly Oriental conformation and fine head with wide-set vivid green eyes, the true Russian Blue is a real aristocat. Nor should we ignore the Japanese Bobtail—long-legged, white with black or red patches here and there, said to be intelligent, friendly, loyal and to *love* swimming! Extremely rare even in Japan, the chances of finding one in the UK are fairly remote but there are now a number of them in the USA. Better perhaps to look for a native-born Manx cat, which is usually completely tail-less and comes in all varieties of colour. It is possibly best-looking as a tabby, and though it has a short body, its long back legs enable it to run very fast. A Manx is said to be courageous, affectionate and a good mouser.

Just two more unusual varieties for you to consider: the Cornish and the Devon Rex, distinguished by their curly and wavy coats. They first appeared as mutations in farm cats in the counties after which they are named in 1950 and 1960. Skilful breeding has now made it possible for almost any colour to be produced, including a Si-Rex. The heads are medium wedge-shaped, with the Cornish having a straight profile and the Devon nose having a marked stop. The bodies are slender, of medium length, the tails long and tapering. Named after the curly-

coated rabbits, they are sometimes called 'poodle' or 'pixie' cats.

And now for the British Shorthair, in all its splended variety of colours. But how does one distinguish a pure-bred animal from one of mixed parentage?

Basically the British Shorthair is a medium-sized, medium-heavy cat, larger if male and lighter if female. The head is broad and well-rounded, ears set well apart, eyes large and round. The legs are strong, tail thick at the base, fairly short, and rounded at the tip, coat firm and dense. He comes in many colours, too many to detail here, and it is the obligatory matching of eye colour to coat colour, symmetrical marking and patterning, which distinguish the aristocratic or at least pure-bred gentleman from the humble moggie. If his stripes don't match, or an extra colour has crept in where it oughtn't, he slides down the social scale at once. So now you know!

Final thought on choosing cats: there are always lots of ordinary non-pedigree kittens in need of a good home, and given lots of tender loving care any one of them will probably grow up to be a good companion and occasional mouser. So unless you seriously desire to have a pedigree pet—as an ornament to your home or the start of an absorbing hobby if you intend to breed from him or her (better a her, to begin with, because looking after a stud cat takes a lot of expertise)—do consider giving house room to a little cross-breed. They can often be stronger, more intelligent, less self-centred, than the aristocats.

Right: The shorthaired tabby is among the most universally loved cats. Many see it as the epitome of The Cat—strong, independent and fearless

Naming Cats

A cat must have a name.

A thing without a name of its own is a non-thing, a nothing. A house . . . a hill . . . a hole in the ground . . . it could be any place, anywhere. Who cares, if one can't put a name to it?

The same goes for people: who is he/she? what's his/her name? That's one of the very first questions. And for animals too, if you want to address them politely—especially domestic ones.

Take cats. If you meet a strange cat and want to get closer you may say 'Hey there, Puss!' If the cat is lonely (unlikely) or hungry (unusual) it will come to you if it thinks you're reasonably attractive and reliable. But it won't be deceived into thinking you're a pal if you've only called it Puss Puss or Puddy Cat: it knows perfectly well that everybody in the world (sorry, in the English speaking world—in France of course they whisper Min Min Minou instead and in the USSR it's Koshka, come home, etcetera), well, everyone who doesn't know them by name, calls cats in general Puss. So it understands you're addressing it and responds if it feels like it—or not if it doesn't. But if you knew its real name, its *given* name, it would feel under much more of an obligation.

Name-giving is a serious responsibility. Especially giving names to cats. It can be done in a flash of inspiration; on the other hand it may take weeks of thought and discussion. Either way, do bear in mind that you're sticking a label on your cat for the whole of his/her life. Try to find something you think he'll like, a name which won't make him feel a fool when shouted out in public.

Naming children is easier. For a start you usually give them more than one name at their christening. Being able to choose whether she prefers to be (say) Jane, Elizabeth or Louise when old enough to care makes life less rigid altogether for a little girl; and a boy endowed with John Ernest Napoleon can be a source of pride to parents and grandparents but still have the liberty of choice. But in spite of Mr. T. S. Eliot (who insisted, in a poem called *The Naming of Cats*, that 'a cat must have THREE DIFFERENT NAMES!'), whoever heard of a cat (outside the Cat Fancy) being given more than one name?

Furthermore humans have a long growing period in which to adapt to their names, grow into them so to speak. Cats tend to arrive in a household, and be named, and there they are. That's who they are and if they don't like it there's sweet cat all they can do about it.

Come to think of that, I knew one cat which did take exception. He was a very fine fellow, the pick of a litter born to a rare and beautiful longhaired mother whose fur was a glowing marmalade colour (but his brothers and sister had coats of many colours, so mother was in disgrace). The rather precious pair of people he went to live with dubbed him Marmaduke, and were at first distressed, then rather insulted, when he refused at all times to acknowledge their greetings. He appeared at mealtimes and ate what was put before him; then he made a habit of either escaping for a quick walk down the road or taking up station on the windowsill of the first floor front and gazing forth. He was evidently thinking quite deeply as well, and making plans, because after about three months he left home. His owners were sad, insulted, demoralised. They blamed themselves though they knew not why; as far as I know they never kept a cat again. I met

ex-Marmaduke quite soon after their loss but couldn't bring myself to tell them. He had found himself a nice new niche with a family only a few streets away, and was blatantly, blissfully happy. When they felt the need to tell him off they shouted Oh *Ginger!* —but otherwise they just called him Ginge . . .

However, not all cats are so resourceful. I know a black and saturnine (caturnine?) fellow whose whimsical owners call him Twinkle. I'm sure his perpetual scowl is one of shame and embarrassment—but he has never quite got up courage to make a change in his life. On the other paw, the daintiest, most

beautiful blue Longhair-used-to-be-called-Persian which lives next door to one of my sons is, for some inexplicable reason, plain Sam.

Lots of cats have descriptive names. For instance Blackie, Snow-ball, Tabitha (Tabby), Fluff, Spot, Smudge and so on. Not terribly exciting or original but both owners and pets feel comfortable with them. In a sense such names are practical too, because if a cat gets lost and is taken to a cat home or a police station there's just a chance that someone in authority may have the nous to guess at a name and so win the poor wandering one's confidence.

We've had two Blackies in our time. When we named the first we didn't feel unenterprising because she came to us as a stray—settled on us, rather—and we had to play a name-guessing game with her. When we suggested *Blackie?* she more or less said 'Yes, That's Me!' so Blackie she was from then on, if not before. When she died, and a little black kitten was given to us to take her place, that became Blackie the Second automatically—and lived to spend eighteen happy years with us, too.

We had a cat called Felix once. I think Felix is a really nice name for a cat: it's almost though not quite

felis, the generic name for all cats (and that includes lions and tigers as well and in Latin it means 'happy'. So call one of yours Felix and you're more or less dubbing him Happy Cat from the moment of his 'christening' (though I've never yet heard of a female cat called Felicia or Felicity—have you?).

A new friend in the country came round the side of the house and into the kitchen for a cup of tea and said 'There's a tiger cat out there, sitting in the long grass watching the birds. Is that one of yours?' Which reminds me that a lot of people appropriately call tabby cats Tiger as well as Tabitha or Tabs.

Both our current cats are tabbies.

But the older one was given the dignified name of Maude because a rather eccentric dear friend surprised us by asking if the new kitten could be named after her. In time Maude the kitten grew up and became Mother Maude, and recently she's become very fond of my sister-in-law who, for inexplicable reasons of her own, calls her Ethel. She's obviously a very adaptable cat, being prepared to answer to two names at once! Maude's daughter— the only one still at home—is as longhaired as Maude is smooth; we've no idea where she gets that from! When she was a kitten she seemed to be just a tiny ball of fluff, light as a feather. We said it so often—Oh, isn't she fluffy, none of

the others are and neither are Grey Daddy or Black Daddy (Maude's then lovers)—that the rhyming Buffy slipped out almost without thought. But it stuck, and fragile, indomitable Buffy has been a good companion and a delight for the past six years.

As I said, it's quite a heavy task, the naming of cats. Possibly one of the best ways is to choose a name to suit temperament, even though that does mean having a little no-name around the house for a while until you get to know what sort of cat he or she seems to be. I've been making some just-in-case lists, in alphabetical order; maybe one of these will suit your new cat to purrfection . . . I hope so.

A

Abacus a calculating cat
Achilles a cat with a weakness
Adam an original cat
Alice a puzzled cat (confused?)
Arthur a kingly cat
Axminster a disgraceful cat

B

Bacchus an orgiastic cat
Backgammon a game cat
Badger a demanding cat
Beaver an industrious cat
Bilker a disreputable cat
Bliss a happy cat

C

Carol a Christmas cat
Charlie a darling cat
Chili a superior cat
Chin Chin a bibulous cat
Christopher Columbus an adventurous cat
Crumpet a sexy cat
Chuck a rangy cat

D

Dado a base cat
Dally a flirtatious cat
Decorum a perfect cat
Density a stupid cat
Dhobi a white cat
Dilly an irresolute cat
Dodger an artful cat
Don a studious cat

E

Ebony a black cat
Elegy a poetic cat
Ellington a musical cat
Encore a repetitious cat
Epitome a concise cat
Ernest a resolute cat
Extempore a resourceful cat

F

Facade a deceitful cat
Fatso a jolly cat
Faux Pas a clumsy cat
Favour a gracious cat
Felix a happy cat
Fidget a restless cat
Flotsam a stray cat
Frolic a cheerful cat

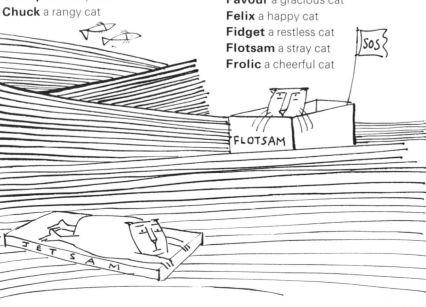

G

Gabble a chatty cat
Galore a fruitful cat
Galahad a courtly cat
Geyser an unpredictable cat
Gloss an ostentatious cat
Goulash a cat of mixed parentage
Grin a Cheshire cat

H

Harmony a gentle cat
Headache a cat with problems
Hebe a beautiful cat
Hector a brave cat
Heidi a modest cat
Help a reliable cat
Holly a prickly cat, easily annoyed
Hoodlum a delinquent cat

33

Idiosyncrasy a nonconforming cat
Idle a lazy cat
If a doubtful cat
Imbroglio a muddled cat
Impetus an inspiring cat
IOU a borrowed cat
Ivy a clinging cat

Jackpot a lucky cat
Jasper a precious cat
Jazz an exciting cat
Jenkins a convivial cat
Joss an idolised cat
Jubilee a celebration cat
Justice a fair-minded cat

Kanga a jumpy cat
Karma a spirited cat
Keeper a watchful cat
Ketchup a saucy cat
Kibosh an absurd cat
Kind Regards a courteous cat
Kung Fu a martial cat

Lanolin a smooth cat
Larceny a thieving cat
Largo a greedy cat
Lemon a sour puss
Lent an abstemious cat
Likelihood an optimistic cat
Liturgy a church cat

Mafia an unscrupulous cat
Mangold a country cat
Masher an amorous cat
Mellow an amiable cat
Mercy a kind cat
Minister an authoritative cat
Modesty a demure cat

Pickle a mischievous cat
Pounce a surprising cat

Q

Quail a cowardly cat
Quaker a friendly cat
Quartz a hardhearted cat
Query a curious cat
Quibble an argumentative cat
Quiff a vain cat
Quiver a nervous cat

N

Napoleon an imperious cat
Narcissus a vain cat
Nausea a sickening cat
Nemesis a vengeful cat
Neuter a castrated cat
Nick a devilish cat
Niobe a sad cat
Nod a sleepy cat

O

Obbligato a creative cat
Obsequy a respectful cat
Oedipuss a cat with a mother complex
Officer an important cat
Oracle a prophetic cat
Opium a soothing cat
Orpheus a musical cat
Oyster a taciturn cat

P

Palaver a busy cat
Paragon an excellent cat
Parody a copy cat
Peach a pretty cat
Perfidy a deceitful cat

R

Rascal a disobedient cat
Rhodes a scholarly cat
Rigmarole a mixed-up cat
Robinson a solitary cat
Romeo a romantic cat
Roundelay a stout cat
Rummy a cat who's a bit of a card

S

Sage a wise cat
Saturday Morning a holiday cat
Scrabble a destructive cat
Scrooge a mean cat
Simon a simple cat
Sober a temperate cat
Sorry a penitent cat
Synch an adaptable cat

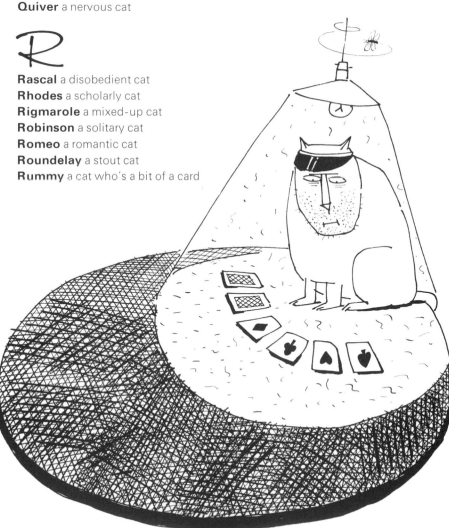

T

Taboo an unspeakable cat
Tango a dancing cat
Tedium a boring cat
Temperance a moderate cat
Tiddlywinks a jolly cat
Tovarich a comradely cat
Trotsky an activist cat
Tuppeny a trifling cat

U

Ultima a limited cat
Ulysses a wandering cat
Umbrage a resentful cat
Uproar a noisy cat
Utopia a dream cat
Uxor a much married cat

V

Vagary a whimsical cat
Velvet a smooth cat
Verity a truthful cat
Venture a brave cat
Vim a vigorous cat
Virtue a good cat
Vogue an elegant cat

W

Welcome a hospitable cat
Whereabouts a roaming cat
Willow an elusive cat
Winsome a lovable cat
Wizard a magic cat
Wolfgang a virtuoso cat
Worry a neurotic cat
Worship a respectful cat

X

X Ray an enquiring cat
X an anonymous cat

Y

Yale a secure cat
Yarborough an unlucky cat
Yeast a bubbly cat
Yoghourt a healthy cat
Yogi a wise cat
Yoyo a playful cat

Z

Zeal a keen cat
Zen a meditative cat
Zero a last-minute cat
Zither a harping cat
Zoom a fast cat

Well-behaved Cats

Cats like to get their own way, as everyone knows. So it may seem over-confident to say that they can be trained to be mannerly and well-behaved. But I'm sure that they can. Only it isn't so much a matter of training as of mutual understanding and co-operation: not only the cats being trained but also their owners.

Take for example litter boxes. The happiest cats are those which have access to outdoor toilet facilities, that's to say if they want to spend a penny or more they can get out through a permanently ajar window or a cat-flap in window or door, find a suitable place with loose earth or sand which they can scratch about in to make a hole, perform in that, cover it up carefully, then come back indoors feeling virtuous and much, much better.

The alternative to this happiest of states is the litter-box system. A box should be shallow, rectangular and preferably plastic because that's easy to clean. It should be about 18″×12″ (45×30 cm approx) by 3″ (about 8 cm) deep, and should be filled to within about an inch, or $2\frac{1}{2}$ cm, of the top with a proprietary cat litter (better than sand or earth because it's got built-in deodoriser

and antiseptic) and kept in the same private but easily accessible place at all times. Owners should check on its condition first thing in the morning and last thing at night, removing soiled litter, giving any which remains a good stir and a shake, topping up with new. It's a good idea to put the box on a sheet or two of newspaper if there's room, so that if the cat scratches in the litter and it overflows on to the floor it's more easily contained and swept up. If all this sounds a lot of bother it isn't really, once you've got into the routine. And expense? Well that's just something you have to put up with if you can't provide a garden lavatory. You can cut it down a bit if you buy the litter in the outsize sacks available at some supermarkets.

Contrary to what anti-cat people say, cats very rarely make messes indoors. Obviously if a cat is shut in a room for any length of time, something sooner or later is going to give, but most cats will go to busting point rather than piddle in the wrong place. If the worst does happen, what you must never do is smack him or shout at him. He couldn't help what he did—if you left him shut in it's more your fault than his anyway—just clean up after him, making certain that no residual smell is left (this is not only for your nose's sake but also to remove any possibility of him thinking it's an o.k. place to do it again). Explain quietly about always going outside or in the litter box, and leave it at that.

Most kittens are house-trained by their mothers. But if you acquire a new one which isn't, having left home too young, he should be put on the litter box first thing in the morning and again after each meal. He'll soon understand what it's for. And if by any chance you see him settling down elsewhere to do his business, he should be picked up quickly and put on the box—that should help him to get the idea. If an accident occurs speak seriously and firmly about it of course, but never scold and never smack—that would only frighten and confuse him, possibly setting the training programme back for weeks.

One expert says that an owner can help by dipping a finger in warm water when she puts the kitten on the litter box, and gently stroking the little creature's tummy and rear end several times; her explanation is that if the mother cat were in charge she would be licking her baby to stimulate the urinary/defaecating mechanisms, and the warm wet human finger is a substitute for this. Mother cats also teach their kittens to cover their excreta—a welcome and hygienic habit which in fact goes right back to their ancestors' life in the wild when it was essential to leave no smells which might attract predators.

Well-mannered cats never pester people to feed them. Actually this is not just good manners but a matter of pride and dignity: a cat expects to be fed regularly and well, so

what's the point of grovelling for something which is bound to come anyway? But in this again the cat's owner must act responsibly. Mealtimes must be adhered to—if not rigidly then as closely as possible—and meals should always be of the standard to which a cat has become accustomed. If you are late with a meal, the most the majority of civilised cats will do is assemble themselves in the appointed place and wait, and watch you when you do appear, and wait . . . and watch, and watch. And if all that patient, hard-done-to watching doesn't get you down and make you resolve never to be late with supper again, you're a tougher cat-lover than I am!

Titbits are different. They might happen at any time of day, as an unexpected treat. But as a general rule they're not a good thing because they spoil the appetite for regular meals. Cats shouldn't pester for them either, and most don't. If owners are weak and allow wicked habits to start—such as Buffy Butter I suppose, which you'll find mentioned in the Hungry Cats chapter—

the important thing to remember is that they must be prepared to put up with the habit and acknowledge that it was all their fault from the beginning—and not the cat's.

Cats can be very destructive, if not corrected firmly. They have a definite need to scratch with their claws, and knead with their paws. This is in order to clean the claws and keep them trim, and also to exercise the shoulder muscles. If they do all this out of doors no one really notices, but when the habit is brought indoors it can be devastating in terms of ripped up furniture and carpets. As always with cats, patience and understanding are what you need, however difficult these may be to achieve when your favourite things are being destroyed before your very eyes. Best of all, of course, is a garden in which there are trees, or a wooden fence, or gateposts. All of these are convenient objects to scratch against. If you haven't any of them you might go looking for an old rough log somewhere which you could prop up in the porch; your cats will then either walk past it and ignore it, implying

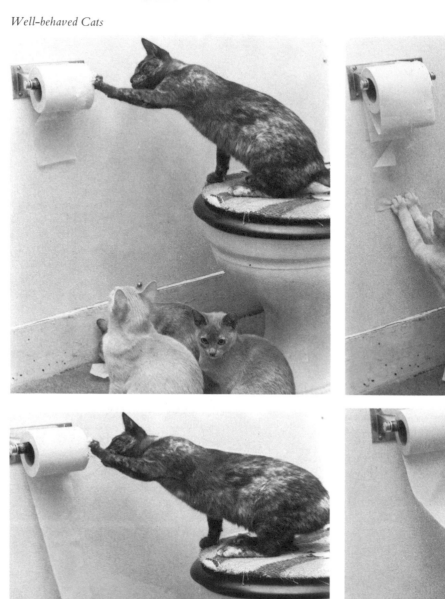

that you must be going a bit loco bringing home chunks of old wood, or leap upon it with cries of joy (you should be so lucky!).

Pet shops sell 'scratching posts' made of wood or cork or pieces of carpet stuck to a rigid base, all recommended for fixing up in the home. Some cats enjoy these, others ignore them. I've known desperate owners who first bought a scratching post, which was left completely unscratched, then a catnip mouse which they painstakingly rubbed all over the post in order to attract the cats. Guess what, that didn't work either. I've known people who lost all dignity and started scratching at the posts themselves, as an example! And even people so brash and insensitive as to take a cat by his paws and try to show him how to scratch. Did it do them any good? It did not—*and* their cats didn't think any the better of them.

In time the habit may disappear, or a post of some sort be accepted. Perhaps one leg of the kitchen table could be agreed upon? Keep up the pressure with gentle reproof rather than shouts and throwing things. Plenty of pepper sometimes helps if you don't mind the look and sneeziness of it in little heaps all over the house. (Pepper's cheaper than furniture, after all.) Please *never* get so desperate as to consider having your cat(s) de-clawed—it's true that some vets will do it, but it surely amounts to amputation, ten times over, of a part of the animal vital to its health and security. The pain can't help but be considerable, and the psychological effect totally demoralising.

Left: Some have enquiring minds, others just like encouraging their friends to get into mischief . . .

The other kind of scratching can be troublesome too, unless you and your cat come to an understanding about it early on in your friendship. If you are friends, the last thing he wants to do is to hurt you. He loves and trusts you, there's no need for him to take hostile action against you. But just occasionally deep-buried instincts may take over— if he's frightened or in pain, for example. And at such times it's up to you to take precautions. Don't pick him up without wearing thick gloves—otherwise it will be your fault if he scratches you, not his.

Similarly, as already mentioned in the chapter on the Nature of Cats, never play with a kitten with just your hands, or he'll come to think of them as playthings which can be attacked and bitten or scratched. That's all very well in a kitten with tiny teeth and claws, which scarcely hurt at all, but what about when he's older and much stronger? Playthings from the beginning should be a twist of paper, a ball, a leaf, a length of string. And what about a scrummy cat-nip mouse?

Can you train a cat to be obedient, to stop if you say no, to come when you call? Yes, you can. Say 'No' firmly but not roughly, never shout or slap. If he keeps on doing whatever it is, withhold the sunshine of your smile, speak disapprovingly and remove him from the room for a while. He'll learn, he's not stupid. And because (*if* you have the proper sort of cat/human relationship) he really quite likes you, he'll want to do things that please you rather than annoy.

Of course cats can be very obtuse, and sometimes when you invite them to sit on your lap they just give you a disdainful look and maybe even turn their back—but in such cases you've usually asked at an unsuitable moment, or done something to annoy them a few minutes ago even though you didn't realise, so their disobedience and ungraciousness is fully justified. Well, they think it is, anyhow!

Having a cat come to your call can be marvellous; especially when he hears your voice and you can see him coming from a distance, bounding over the ground so effortlessly with his coat shining in the sunshine. As he gets nearer to you he will slow down a little for the sake of dignity but then speeds up at the final approach with tail up, eyes alert and a greeting 'Prrrp' of pleasure. It's wonderful, too, to open the door late at night and say 'Pudd, Pudd, Pudd' and to hear an answering scamper and a scrape and a thud as he jumps down from a wall or a tree before you make out his shape coming towards you out of the darkness. He'll rub against your legs, purring throatily in delight at being asked to come in and sit by the fire.

But perhaps that isn't obedience, after all. Perhaps it's just friendship.

Well-groomed Cats

Some folk never put brush to cat in all the years of their association. These people say that cats can look after themselves, *prefer* to look after themselves, and who are mere humans to interfere?

This may be just all right for a tough, resilient, self-reliant, mixed-parentage Shorthair, which doesn't have to worry much about fur balls in his tummy, doesn't notice fleas and doesn't care all that much if he acquires the odd burr or teazle which has to be painstakingly licked out of his tail; but for many domestic cats it just isn't good enough. In fact it almost amounts to neglect.

Grooming doesn't take long. The secret is that it should happen daily if the cat is a Longhair, because otherwise uncomfortable, unsightly and unsanitary mats can form. Once formed, they can literally be agony to get rid of. And if the cat's a Shorthair it should be at least once a week. Grooming isn't just a matter of brushing and combing, either. It should include a quick skin inspection each time—in case any fleas or ticks have attached themselves to your pet—and a check-up of eyes and ears to make sure they aren't runny or clogged with wax.

A full-grown cat which has never been groomed before may well object if he suddenly finds himself the subject of so much attention; you may find it difficult, if not impossible, to make him keep still and take part. He may want out straight away and make his wishes clear with tooth and claw. If he shapes like this, don't try to detain him. But do repeat the attempt day after day after day, accompanying it with soothing words, at the same time and in the same place until he gets used to it. Cats *love* ritual.

While you're exploring the situation in this way, let the merest touch or two of the comb or the brush be enough; never insist on continuing for longer than your cat can stand. When he indicates that he's ready to be off, do co-operate by lifting him gently down from the table you've stood him on for grooming. Tell him he's been very good and he's looking beautiful, and let him go. Very slowly, you'll find that even the most suspicious and nervous cat begins to enjoy his grooming sessions. First, because he's the focus of attention, and cats love that; second, because the very gentle combing and/or brushing sensation is so delicious; and finally, because when it's all over he feels clean and absolutely spaced-out.

Usually a table is the best place for grooming. This is because you can walk all around it. Preferably it should have an unpolished surface and be of a good height so that you don't have to stoop, and can thus avoid backache. Lay out your grooming tools close to hand and call your cat. If he's used to grooming he'll probably be ready and waiting; if not, he may have to be found, picked up, stroked and talked to gently as he is placed on the table. Always start grooming with a few moments of all-over stroking by hand: not only does this give your cat great pleasure but it also enables you to locate any trouble spots which may be present—a tangle, an incipient mat, a tender place, a bite—and you'll know then to avoid them with brush and comb but give them special attention later.

When the cat is calm, start the grooming proper. For this you need good quality steel combs with no rough points or jagged protrusions. For Longhairs there should prefer-

Right: Il faut souffrir . . . (well no, not really—but if not, why look so grumpy about it?) . . . pour etre belle . . .

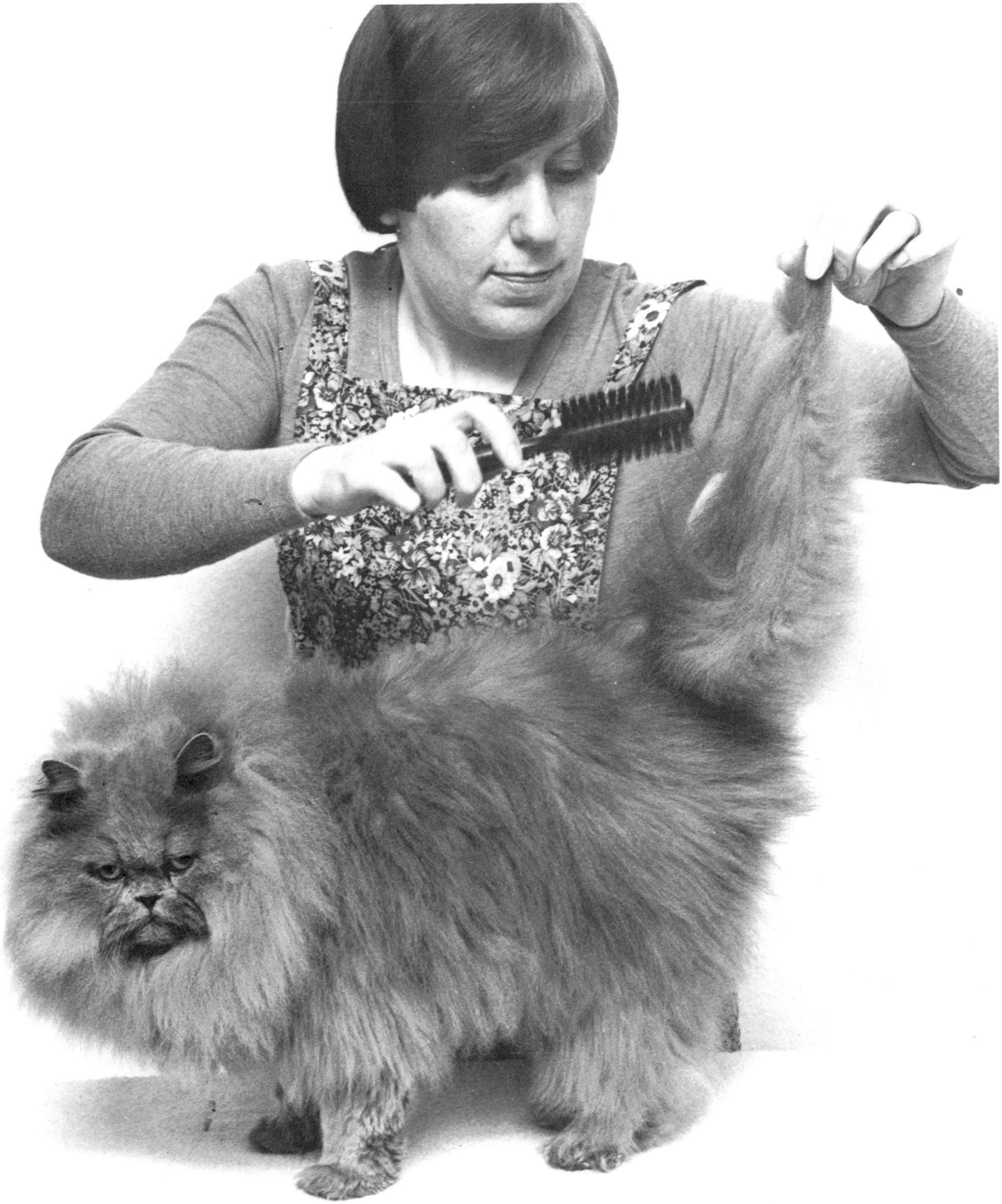

ably be two sizes of long-toothed comb, one with teeth wide apart and another with teeth set closer. Smaller-toothed combs are better for Shorthairs. For both you will need a good quality brush (bristle rather than nylon), cotton wool swabs to clean eyes and ears, and a pair of blunt-nosed surgical scissors in case a mat has to be dealt with.

It's sensible to groom the various parts of the body in the same order every time, so that the cat knows what to expect. For example, you might start with the back of the neck. This is pleasant for him and not in the least frightening. Continue round the neck and chest which he'll very likely enjoy too; next move on to the back, which is another pleasure area. Then go on to the thighs which are easy enough on the outside but a more delicate task (which must *not* be neglected) on the inside where the skin is sensitive. Proceed to the tummy, which needs great care for fear of hurting delicate nipples, on to the front legs both outside and inside, and then finish with rear-end trousers and tail. Always be very gentle, very patient; do avoid knocking boney bits with the comb or dragging it harshly too close to the skin. Stop at once if your cat makes serious objections or shouts at you—otherwise you'll only put him off grooming for life.

The best way to comb—the most pleasurable and least painful for your cat, plus being most effective —is to use one of your hands to hold and manipulate the comb and the other to stroke and firm the cat's

Right: If burrs catch, or 'mats' form, in your cat's coat, cut—don't tug—them out. Far right: A shorthair can be groomed with either a small-toothed comb or a brush but usually only a brush is necessary

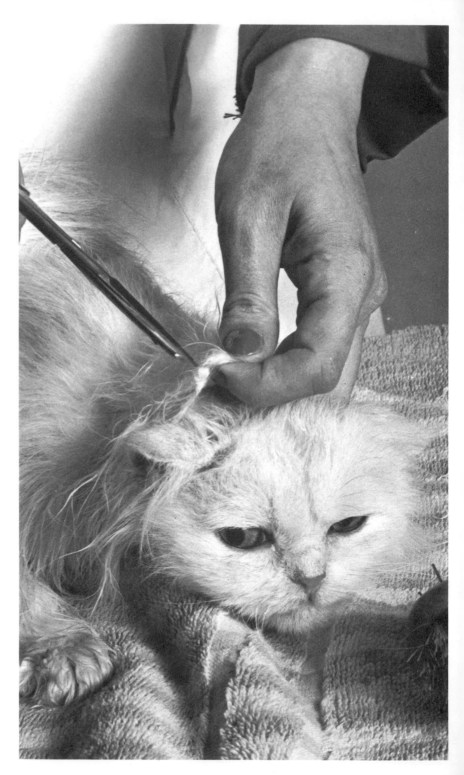

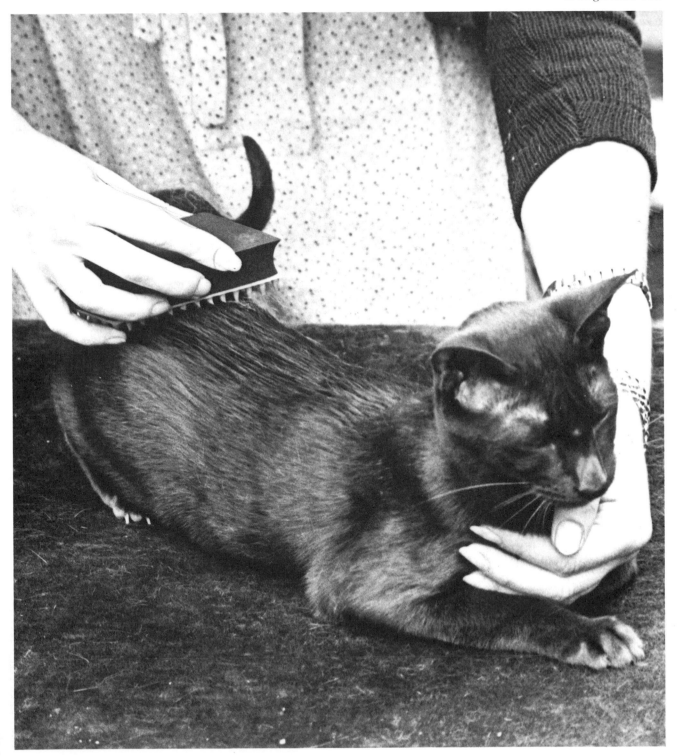

skin—which, being loose, could otherwise wrinkle and get nicked. The main grooming of a Longhair should be done with combs; brushing to put on a shine and to remove loose hairs should be the last stage. A Shorthair may only need brushing most of the time—but do remember to part the hair each week and check the condition of the skin.

Next comes a quick look at the eyes. If they're healthy, leave well alone but if there's any sign of discharge they should be gently cleansed with cotton wool dipped in warm, sterile (boiled) water or a proprietary (specially for cats) eye lotion. Any continuing discharge should be treated by your vet.

And ears. These should be checked weekly and, if necessary, dusted with a proprietary anti-canker powder or dabbed inside with lotion (also anti-canker) or wiped out with olive oil on a twist of cotton wool. Please don't probe deeply, though; you'll only risk compacting the wax. And *never* use any oil but a vegetable one, because the cat will surely lick it out and

ingest it. As for the eyes, if an unhealthy or distressing condition persists it should be seen and dealt with by the vet. He will probably clear it up very quickly with anti-biotics, costing you a small fee but saving your cat a lot of suffering and you a lot of anxiety.

For a cat in good condition, used to regular grooming and with no special problems, the whole process of daily grooming should take no more than five minutes or so from the first pick-up to put-down-again-with-praise. It should be a pleasure to both pet and owner. However, if by unfortunate chance your cat develops a mat—a tangled clump of hair which just won't comb apart—you must disperse it as soon as possible and this will take extra time. Don't persist in trying to comb the mat out, because it hurts. You know how you would feel!

The solution is to cut it, very gently and very carefully, using blunt surgical scissors, never cutting towards the cat's delicate skin but always away from it. If you place the lower blade upright on the skin,

blunt side down, pointing into the mat, you can then push slightly forward and at the same time bring the blades together and cut. This should result in a slight break in the mat and an easing of the tugging sensation which the cat must be suffering. Another two or three similar cuts and the mat should disintegrate. But do work slowly, and be careful. Do a little one day and a little more the next, if the cat is very nervous. And it goes without saying that two people are better than one for this job, one to hold the cat and the other to deal with the mat. But the cat should trust you both equally. Wear gloves!

There's another problem which sometimes arises. You may find that your cat has stepped in oil or tar; if so, this must be removed as soon as possible. Otherwise he could poison himself if he tried to lick it off. Never, *never* use paraffin or petrol! A small amount of methylated spirits is the best solvent, on a bit of cotton wool. Wipe gently until all trace of the tar has gone. If your cat is so dumb as to come into contact with wet paint—well, it may not be his fault but most cats are usually quick to avoid such stuff—the best thing is to cut off the painted fur. It will soon grow again and, unless he's a show cat whose every hair counts, that's much better for him than having to inhale the amount of meths needed to dissolve the paint.

Some cats quite like water, and some owners actually do bathe their cats. Experts say that a bath does a cat no harm, though not all cats would agree. If your cat manages to get really filthy, or heavily con-

If it's necessary to clean round the eyes, use a sterile cotton swab

taminated with farmyard muck, and can't cope (though once again most cats have much too much sense to get into such a situation) then a warm bath plus a baby shampoo may be the only solution. Rather you than me! Never use strong soap and never get soap or shampoo in his eyes.

Dry him in fluffy warm towels, unless he has nerves of steel—in which case you might try using the hairdryer on him. Warning: if he likes it, he'll probably become addicted to its lovely warm breath and soothing purr, and demand to be bathed and dried once a week! (I know of one cat who loves to be hoovered!)

Some show cats are bathed quite frequently, especially if their coats are white or very pale in colour. It's usually done a few days before the show, to give the natural oils in the coat time to re-establish themselves. Some owners plug the cat's ears with cotton wool, to make quite sure that no water gets into them, and experts warn that pedigree cats in particular catch cold quite easily so should be kept indoors after a bath until they are completely dry again.

Footnote: some owners cut their cats' nails, and instructions are given in several cat books I've read. I've never tried it on ours because they've always had plenty of outdoors to play in and find things to keep their nails under control, so I've no experience of how easy or difficult it is. But I should think you'd have to be very skilful and very patient, and your cat very trusting and forbearing. I suggest you check with your vet before attempting it.

Miss Puss frequently prefers to be her own hair stylist/manicurist—and the salon is always open

Healthy Cats

Most kittens are born healthy. You don't often see a mother-to-be cat looking starved or ill-treated—most are far too adept at finding a good home and an obedient owner! By the time the kittens come along they have the best possible chance of a good start in life.

So the odds are that when you take over your first kitten he will be a clean, well-nourished, contented little animal; alert, adventurous and amiable. He will be ready to make friends with you, to live with you as an equal, to rule you if he can. He will expect to attain and maintain a high degree of independence; he will want to come and go as he pleases as soon as he is old and strong enough. But in spite of this he will need your support and your loving care if he's going to make the most of his life.

Whether or not he's prepared to admit it, *you* are going to be his most important person. You provide his home, his bed, his food; you open doors and windows so that he can come in and go out; you groom him—or should do—you organise his regular meal-times. You are there when he needs you, you talk to him and he can talk to you—even if he can't always make himself understood very clearly. He is your responsibility, in fact—and all that he is, and is going to be, depends on you.

Above all, you must help him guard that most precious gift of good health with which he was born. Because although coming from a strong and fit mother and having a good home helps a lot, there are bound to be times when you'll need to seek professional advice on his behalf. So as soon as

you become a cat owner you should make acquaintance with a vet.

Experience has taught me not to contact just any vet. Most are kind and conscientious, but some do better with cats than with dogs, with budgies than with hamsters, with cows than sheep. I've even met a vet (just socially I'm glad to say) who claimed that he didn't like animals at all! The best way to choose your vet is to go by personal recommendation. Look out for clean, happy, cheerful cats and if you manage to nobble the owner of one speak words of praise first then ask the key question 'Do you mind telling me which vet you take him to?' Most cat lovers will be only too pleased to pass on this information, when you explain why you asked. And after a week or two of such canvassing around the district—although a few people may think you're mildly eccentric—you'll hopefully have what you want: the names of two or three vets who do well by cats. Now it's

Left: The tree is nature's scratching post—but an upright pole, inside or out, would do as well provided it had a roughish surface. Right: Face to face—puss to puss, as Americans would say. Vet and patient inspect each other

48

just a question of picking the one nearest your home, to save journey time in an emergency.

Your first visit will be for a shot of feline enteritis vaccine, and this should happen as soon as possible after acquiring your kitten. (It's possible of course that the breeder will have had the first vaccination done already—enquire when collecting the kitten. But if not, it should be an urgent first task.)

Ideally a kitten should have its first shot at nine weeks old and another at twelve, and it's now possible to combine the anti-enteritis immunization with another against feline influenza. Both these virus diseases are common in cats, and can be fatal, but proper preventative action at an early age should give complete immunity. You can ensure that this continues by taking your pet along to the vet for an annual booster

shot—it doesn't hurt, doesn't make him feel ill, and could save his life.

That first visit, though, will also give both you and your cat the opportunity to meet the vet and see how you get on together. All veterinary surgeons receive the same basic training, so you needn't worry much about one being more skilful than another; your cat should receive the same high standard of care wherever you go. But it's important too that the animal should like—or at least be prepared to tolerate—the person who's going to have to treat him if he's ill, and equally important that you yourself should find the vet sympathetic and conscientious. If you really don't, then make a change before it's too late. But don't do that frivolously or for the wrong reasons—not, for instance, just because you don't agree with a recommended treatment. You're the cat's concerned owner but the vet is the professional

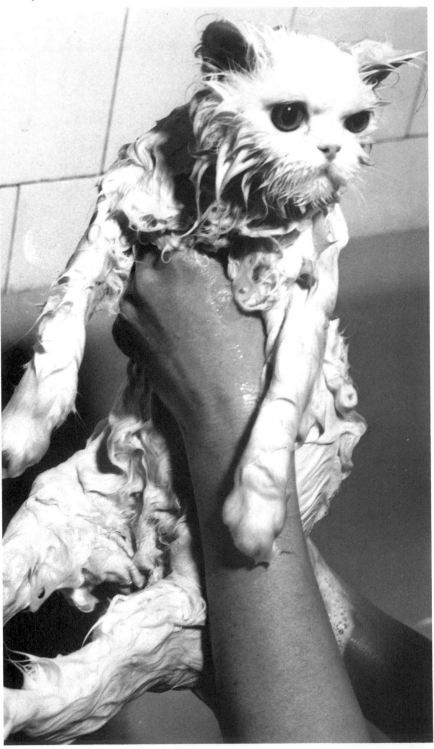

and knows a lot more about animal health than you do.

One word of warning here: as I said, most kittens are born healthy —but if you get yours from an 'animal shelter', or a pet shop, it's just possible that it may have been in contact with infection. So if it seems at all listless or off food, do consult your vet at once.

A healthy cat should eat well but not be over greedy; he should sleep well—don't worry if he sleeps a lot by day, he's probably awake and busy half the night when you're snoring! When awake he should be alert and interested in what's going on around him. His eyes should be bright and clear, his nose and ears clean and without discharge; his teeth should be white and clean-looking, gums and tongue pink. His fur should be full, smooth and glossy. He shouldn't be too fat (make allowances on this for a cat which is 'getting on a bit') or too skinny; his paws and claws should be in good order and his jumping up or down machinery should work without him thinking about it—no effort at all either way. He shouldn't have diarrhoea but shouldn't be constipated either; he shouldn't itch, or scratch unduly (ideally not at all).

If he does happen to be attacked by any kind of parasite, he needs help as quickly as you can give it. Fleas, lice, mites and ticks, all of which obviously cause itching followed by scratching, can easily be identified and dealt with at home, chiefly by dusting the cat with

Left: Mee-ooow!! It's not every feline's favourite treatment, but a show cat—or a particularly dirty moggie—may need a gentle bath from time to time. Right: Most cats eat grass sometimes, either as an aid to digestion or as an emetic which helps to expel furballs

a proprietary powder—we find Sherley's No-Scratch very effective—then working it well into the fur before brushing it out. Bedding, cat baskets—anything the cat may have sat on—should be treated at the same time. Treatment should be repeated routinely at regular intervals to avoid reinfestation.

Skin troubles usually come to your notice when your cat scratches a great deal, or when tiny sores appear and the coat starts to come out in patches. This may be due to the fact that you have not got rid of all fleas, etc., but it can also be due to many other causes, so see your vet.

Mange is not seen in cats, except as a variety which affects the head and ears only. Ringworm, however, is quite common and as it is so contagious to humans, it can be serious. Your vet will advise on treatment, but of course the utmost care and scrupulous cleanliness are essential, together with thorough disinfecting of all the cat's bedding. Don't ever use DDT, or anything containing it, when treating parasites or allied conditions on your cat. Use a proprietary powder, specially formulated for cats and dogs, or ask your vet for a special prescription.

Round worms can make young kittens quite ill, so start treatment as soon as your new pet arrives with a preparation obtainable from the vet, the chemist or a pet shop. Modern remedies are quite palatable and easy to administer, and treatment should be continued at regular intervals, as advised, until the kitten is at least one year old, just to make sure all is well.

Tape worms more often affect adult cats, and are more difficult to remove. But your vet will probably be able to supply you with an effective treatment.

A healthy cat never sweats,

according to the well-known wildlife vet David Taylor. In his book *The Cat: An Owner's Maintenance Manual*, he says that cats lose heat by radiation from their body surfaces, which are larger compared with their bulk than those of bigger creatures. Cats sometimes pant, he goes on to say, but never (in health) slobber. (Mind you, I know a cat who dribbles at the sight of food for humans when he knows he might be given a tiny piece if fate is kind. But I suppose that's different!)

David Taylor has an interesting technical explanation of purring in the same book: he says that it is caused by the vibration of blood in a large vein in the chest cavity. Apparently 'where the vein passes through the diaphragm . . . contraction of the muscles nips the blood flow and sets up oscillations, the sounds of which are magnified by the air-filled bronchial tubes and windpipe'. Newborn kittens feel this vibration, and know that Mum is there, though they can't yet see her. He also says that cats may purr when in pain or nervous, as well as when they're pleased and contented.

Later on in the book, discussing possible uses of the cat's whiskers as a help to negotiating obstacles in the dark (no one's quite sure whether this is what they're for or not), David Taylor says that because they are so highly sensitive to vibration cats seem to have a built-in 'early-warning system' and he notes that peasants on the slopes of earthquake-prone Mount Etna are said to keep cats as early tremor detectors! 'When the fireside tom ups and makes for the door hell-for-leather for no apparent reason, the human occupants follow hot foot!' I can almost match that one: during a time of constant bombing, when one practically lived in an air raid shelter,

cats would venture out during lulls in the attack but would frequently return at high speed even though all still appeared to be peaceful—usually to be followed only seconds later by the aircraft which they had heard long before we did.

Possibly because of this extreme sensitivity, even the healthiest cat can appear to be nervous at times, testing both the atmosphere and the company (especially if it includes a stranger) with great care, and disappearing from view if it seems to be dangerous or unsympathetic. So it wouldn't be right to say that a healthy cat is calm and self-possessed at all times, because he isn't.

A cat is such an independent character that it's difficult to judge his state of *mental* health, but although you can't expect too much of his social behaviour he should on the whole be reasonably well-behaved in company if he elects to join in. He should not be too much scared by loud noises or strange people (though if he prefers to hide in the airing cupboard on Guy Fawkes's Night that's just common sense). He certainly shouldn't spit, or scratch people, without gross provocation; and he oughtn't to be continually getting into fights the results of which (torn ears, punctured skin on other parts of the body) could damage his health and spoil his beauty. Mind you, most fighting is done by tomcats competing either for territorial rights or a lady's favours, and you can stop that for ever, almost certainly making his life longer as well as healthier—though from his point of view it may never be so exciting again—by having him neutered. More about that in a later chapter.

Right: Not even a healthy cat is always calm . . .

Pregnant Cats

Female cats only allow themselves to be mated when they are in season, or 'heat' as the oestrus period is called. But this happens so frequently during spring and summer—and even occasionally in autumn and winter too, against all the rules—that to a distracted owner it can seem as if it's going on all the time. Either you have to keep the cat firmly indoors during her season, or let her out and take the consequences—usually three or four of them—at least twice a year.

How can you tell when she's coming into season? Partly because there's a distinct swelling of the vulva (the second hole down from the base of her tail, to be specific), partly because Madam becomes extra-affectionate and rather restless, her appetite for food increases and she has, although you may not notice it because she keeps herself so clean, a slight discharge from that swollen vulva. However above all you'll know when it happens by the noise she makes. She'll call; how she'll call! 'Come and get me!' she howls—and all the male cats for miles around hasten to oblige. You'll be embarrassed for her, and maybe a little afraid. But don't be: she'll choose the one she fancies

most—or if she's a really shameless hussy, more than one—and over the next day or four will probably mate several times. Then her season will end and the toms will hear another call and depart.

If you truly want a house full of kittens, which will soon grow into cats and repeat the whole cycle, and you are sure you can either care for them properly all the years of their lives or can find good homes for them all, then you'll allow nature to take its course. If you don't and aren't and can't, please read the next chapter, which is about neutering cats. So it alters their whole lifestyle—yes, it does. But surely that is better than bringing all those unwanted kittens into the world?

If you are, or hope to become, a breeder of pedigree cats with ambitious plans for producing a champion of champions, you will have chosen your queen mother (a mature female cat, already a mother or about-to-be, is technically known as a queen) as a kitten. You should select her consort with equal care and she'll visit him for her mating.

Either way, after mating has taken place, you'll have a satisfied queen on your hands. And in just

over two months, you'll be hearing the patter of tiny paws.

In about four weeks after mating and conception, the mother-to-be's nipples—until now hidden by her fur—will become visible and more prominent. She'll wash them with great care when grooming herself. She'll take to eating for four or maybe five, and by about the sixth week she'll begin to look plumper (maybe earlier if she has already had several litters). Just in case she's picked them up somewhere, a queen should always be wormed between being mated and giving birth—any time up to the sixth week of pregnancy is safe to do it—not only for the sake of her own health but because she could pass on the worm eggs to her newborn kittens. And it's specially important, too, to keep her free from fleas and other such pests.

Where she's going to have the kittens now becomes a family debating point. In the airing cupboard, under the stairs, or on someone's bed perhaps? Though of course if she is a highly-bred pedigree cat,

Right: A queen accepts her king. But after love-making she may turn on her partner—so look out, especially if he's your own prized stud

and her offspring are going to be valuable, you will have already determined where you mean her to produce them—in a convenient warm place, possibly a purpose-built pen in integral garage or utility room, free from draughts, with an infra-red heater in case it's needed and clean bedding; all mod cat con.

Otherwise, though you will probably decide to provide her with a nice strong box of some sort with high sides or a lid to ensure privacy, and an opening on one side only for her to get in and out; and no doubt you'll lovingly line it with a piece of old blanket—or better still newspapers which she can tear up to make her bed as she likes it—she'll just as probably decide to choose her own place for the birth. So make sure you keep an eye on her as the day approaches, so that you know where she is when she finally goes into labour and can help in the unlikely event that anything should go wrong.

Cats usually give birth easily, and our Maude for one used to purr all the time—obviously delighted with herself. Each kitten—there are usually three or four in a litter—is born in the placenta or little sac of thick but nearly transparent membrane in which it grew in the womb and which the queen quickly rips open. She washes her new baby all over, upside down and inside out, almost! She then eats the placenta and is ready for the next member of her family to appear—which may happen in fifteen minutes or not for half an hour or so. During this waiting time she should look— and be—purrfectly content and untroubled. But do peep in on her from time to time, if possible without disturbing her, just to make sure that all is well. If she is straining, and labour has gone on for two hours without a kitten appearing, or for more than half an hour between kittens, one of them may have got stuck in the birth canal and both baby and mother need *urgent* help from the vet.

If you know your cat very well, and she has had kittens before and she trusts you, she may allow you to make her a nice clean bed after they've all arrived, and generally tidy up. But if she shows any sign of resenting it, *please* don't. Otherwise she may decide to move the kittens to a more private place—and

that would be a strain on all of them, not to mention a worry for you.

After the birth what she needs above all is peace and quiet, plenty of rest and the minimum of disturbance. For the first day or two she'll probably want very little to eat, but warm milk or Lactol (made up according to the manufacturer's instructions) should be given as often as she will take it. After a day or two offer her some lightly cooked fish.

Her litter box and a bowl of fresh water should be near to her bed so that she can get out and use the box, and take a drink, without leaving her kittens for more than a few moments. When they are very tiny she'll be most reluctant to leave them, and they'll squeak in protest if she does because they'll miss the comfort her furry, milky body gives.

Very likely all her teats will be in good working order, but every day you should very gently run your (well-washed) fingers over them to make sure that none are hard or painful; if you discover one that isn't quite as it should be, try to ease it with warm cotton wool fomentations, and squeeze it very very gently to encourage the milk to flow; if this doesn't work you should ask the vet's advice because in rare cases a teat can get very painful and have to be lanced. A mother cat will feed her kittens herself for several weeks, but shouldn't be allowed to do so exclusively after the first twenty-eight days or so because—especially if she has four of them—it's quite a strain on her own system. You'll find that she eats heartily during this time! As soon as the kittens are about four weeks old they should be offered a milky drink and a tiny quantity of scraped raw meat (only the lean part) or cooked fish. There's more about feeding kittens in the chapter on Hungry Cats.

It's possible to hand-rear kittens if their mother is tired, or ill, or has more than she can cope with, or if there's a weakling which can't compete with the others for its share at the milk bar. What's necessary is a tremendous supply of patience, a tiny amount of a milky drink well diluted with warm boiled water, and a very small doll's feeding bottle with teat. A medicine dropper can also do the trick.

The perennial question of what to do with kittens you don't want can only be answered by saying don't have them (see Neutering Cats, the next chapter), have them painlessly destroyed as soon as possible after they are born, or find good homes for them. The latter is easier said than done, though sometimes you may be lucky; it's worth stressing the word 'good': you really need to know the people to whom the kitten is going to belong, and be sure that they won't let their dogs chase it or their children tease it.

Having them destroyed is not a very happy experience for anybody, least of all their mother after all the energy and hard work she put in to producing them. She should always be left with at least one kitten to look after. Otherwise her continuing milk supply could cause unpleasant abscesses, quite apart from the fact that she would feel terribly bereft and lonely—and would probably start calling again immediately because all her instincts would tell her to replace the lost kittens as soon as possible.

Left: Sometimes there isn't room at the milk bar, or perhaps mother has died, or rejected her offspring because of ill-health. Surrogate mothers need patience, a tiny feeding bottle and milk warmed to blood heat. Right: Bliss! —the natural way

Neutering Cats

One of the books I read while researching for this one said that a female cat can produce more than a hundred kittens during her lifetime if you allow her a minimum of ten reproductive years. Think that in turn all her female offspring could reproduce themselves a hundred times! The mind boggles at the potential size of their family tree!

If cats were as good to eat as rabbits, doubtless some stony-hearted animal hater would have started purpose-breeding them by now. But fortunately for them their metabolism is such that they just don't put on the kind of weight which would make their carcases a commercial proposition — quite apart from the natural prejudice most people have against eating a friend of the family.

All the same, it's undesirable for their own sake to let cats breed ad lib. Assuming that every four kittens of those hundred mentioned above share a birthday, that's twenty-five pregnancies in a lifetime — which is surely too much for anyone's health. So spaying is essential; that, and the castration of tom cats.

I don't much like having it done. I'm sure that it alters a cat's character and attitude to life, changing his/her

interests, making him more placid (do *you* like placid males?) and her more neurotic. When we had our Maude spayed, after she'd produced five or six families of beautiful kittens for each of which we'd had increasing difficulty in finding good homes, she was depressed for weeks on end. I felt it and I knew it: we'd done what was right for her health and for society at large and for our convenience, but we'd made her desperately unhappy. (And I don't go along with people who say one shouldn't attribute human feelings to animals, either — just look into their eyes anytime and you can tell whether all is well with them or not.) Maude was a real earth mother and she loved conceiving and producing babies; now it was impossible for her to do that any longer, life had lost its meaning. But she got over it, as most of us do get over sorrow and disappointment in time, and years later, much loved and cherished, she's stronger and more beautiful than she would have been if we'd allowed kitten-birth to

Right: Neutering does not inhibit physical communication — touching noses and sniffing one another is the usual mode of greeting among friends and acquaintances

go on draining her strength. And now, instead of having a litter of kittens to boss about from time to time she just rules our whole household.

I've another story, just the opposite. One of Maude's daughters, our beautiful fluffy Buffy, was born a maiden lady if ever I saw one, a vain, elegant, narrow-hipped spinster. In spite of that she allowed herself to be seduced at a very early age by one of the irresistible neighbourhood toms. She hated her pregnancy, shuddered throughout the births, ignored her children (Maude, who as usual had a family of her own on the go, practically took them over), became desperately ill with what the vet eventually diagnosed as a hormone imbalance, nearly died, but to our very great relief, eventually recovered. As soon as possible afterwards, she was spayed. Since then—freed forever from the threat of further kitten-bearing—she has lived happily ever after, more beautiful, more contented and more healthy with every passing year.

So there you go. It's obvious, really, that neutering cats is the only course for responsible owners who can't cope with any more kittens and don't want their toms to impregnate other people's females. The operations must of course be done by a properly qualified vet— that goes without saying—but both spaying and castration are safe and simple nowadays. Spaying, which is done under a general anaesthetic, involves removing both ovaries via a short incision in one flank; the cat can be taken home after twenty-

four hours and should be as active as usual, with a good appetite, almost at once. Stitches are removed in about ten days, and the hair which has been shaved in a small patch around the incision grows back completely in a few weeks. Neutering of a tom under six months old can be done under local anaesthetic; it involves removal of the testicles either surgically or by injection, and there is rarely any subsequent pain. Left with the vet first thing in the morning (no breakfast, please!), Tom can be collected the same evening. Apart from being a model of good behaviour from then on, you hope—no fighting, no spraying—he too should appear to be unchanged. He won't be male any more, of course; but he'll almost certainly be more loving towards you, since he's no longer interested in chasing feline girls.

There are differences of opinion about when is the best time to have female cats spayed. Some say 'Let her have just one litter'—but after our experiences with Maude and Buffy I'm pretty sure that I disagree. If a cat never has kittens she doesn't know what she's missing and her health is never at risk as Buffy's was. So I would advise spaying at from four to six month old, whichever your vet thinks best according to the health and development of the individual animal. On the other hand one American cat expert strongly believes that in order not to disturb her basic sexuality a female should be allowed to go through her first heat before being spayed. There *may* be something in that because I must say I've met some very tomboyish and unfeminine ex-female cats which had had their operations early on in life.

The chaps should, I think, definitely be done good and young. But the same American expert argues for delay to between six and eighteen months 'until the urine changes odor and becomes very pungent' for the same reason— to avoid changing the cat's basic sexuality. Perhaps that is kinder. But the important thing is to get it done—otherwise he will stray after loose women, fight rivals as near as possible to the death and spray your house so comprehensively that only he will want to live there.

Left: Neutered cats are healthy and happy. Stalking prey and creeping stealthily about the greenery remain favourite pastimes. Right: 'I just don't want to know, thanks!'

Sick Cats

However fit a cat may be as a rule, there's always the possibility of sickness or accident catching him unawares. What to do then? Golden rule: if the accident has been a major one, with broken bone(s), deeply punctured or badly torn skin, take him to the vet. Do the same if you suspect that an illness is serious. Immediate treatment for the results of an accident, urgent diagnosis and correct treatment of the illness, is essential if your cat is to be spared further suffering. It's no use hanging about and thinking he may be a bit better tomorrow, let's wait and see. In the meantime he *hurts* (how would you like it if you were him?). When you keep a pet you must be just as prepared for the inconvenience, expense and general hassle of illness as you would be if a human member of the family was smitten.

You've both already made friends with the vet, remember (see the chapter on Healthy Cats), so the face is familiar, the journey is known too, and so are your names. It won't be like taking him to a strange place and thereby increasing his fear and your anxiety. So get yourselves over there as soon as possible for expert advice, and then you'll both feel better. But when what's gone wrong is obviously fairly minor, then by all means cope with it yourself.

Small and shallow wounds, for example, should simply be washed in a weak antiseptic solution (pet shops sell antiseptics specially suitable for animals and it's sensible to keep a bottle in the house). Hair surrounding the wound should be trimmed away if the patient will permit; if not, don't cause further angst by trying. Once it's cleaned up, he/she will no doubt take over and tongue wash the wound until it heals, but you should check it once or twice in the first day or two, to be sure that all is well and there's no sign of infection.

Very slight first degree burns, affecting only the fur and a very small area of skin surface (caused by a spark from a wood fire, perhaps) can be treated by gentle application of Acriflavine or Burnol ointment and then kept covered if possible. If caused by acid, apply a mild solution of bicarbonate of soda in water; for alkaline burns, wash with equal parts of vinegar and water. Because shock, which can be lethal, almost always results from a burning accident, the cat really should see a vet unless the burn is really a very small one.

Ear canker, which can become chronic if not treated, is an itchy, often inflamed and generally unhappy state probably caused in the first place by parasites, an attack of eczema, battle wounds which have failed to heal, or scratching to relieve the original irritation. Symptoms are shaking of the head and incessant scratching, in later stages an unpleasant smell and/or discharge; also a dislike of having the head and ears touched. Treatment by proprietary canker lotion is effective in the early stages and a canker powder is available too which not only helps to relieve itching but prevents recurrence if dusted into the ears regularly for a week or two after the outbreak. Don't attempt to wash out the ears with antiseptic, and don't poke about inside them: if the canker persists, go to the vet.

Cats do not catch colds, but they can show cold symptoms—they sneeze, get a sore throat, run at the eyes and nose, sometimes cough as well—and this way indicate more serious trouble (cat flu, for instance)

Right: Most vets welcome a little help from owners: familiar hands and a loved voice can help the patient to relax

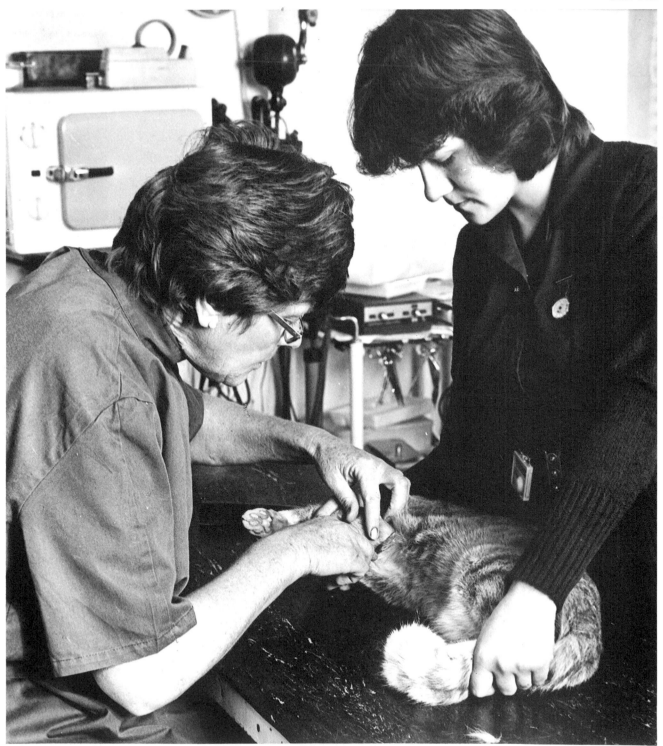

especially if a high temperature develops, so do consult your vet as soon as possible. He will advise on treatment but you can help, of course, by cossetting the invalid a little. Keep him indoors (cat litter box needed now)—preferably in a warm, draught-free room—and give favourite foods to tempt the appetite.

If your cat chokes on a bone or other obstruction he will possibly be able to cope with the situation himself, gulping and retching until he manages to dislodge whatever it is. If he can't, and is obviously miserable and in pain, one person alone can't help very much—but two just might. Both should don thick gloves as protection against scratches and bites. One of them

should wrap the cat securely in an old coat or rug; the other should open his mouth (the cat's!), hold it open, peer within, and if possible extract the offending object with the fingers or a blunt-nosed forceps. I stress blunt-nosed—anything else could do more harm than good.

Cats which are receiving a balanced diet rarely suffer from constipation. If you notice yours straining over his litter box it may indicate bladder troubles, which can be very serious. See your vet at once. But if you live in a flat and your pet doesn't get much exercise, you should be extra careful about diet, and it's a good idea to buy him some toys—one of the best for exercise is a catnip mouse on the

end of a string which you can pull around for him to catch—and make sure he plays with them. Organise a couple of five- or ten-minute playing sessions in which you too take part daily. If you really think it's necessary, give him a few drops of liquid paraffin if he'll take it, but *don't* let this become a habit. *Never* dose him with castor oil, it's far too drastic.

Diarrhoea can also occur; sometimes it's a symptom of another illness which must of course be investigated, but it can also be due to dirty feeding dishes, a cold, or old age. The best way to cope is to fast the cat for a day, then give something light and bland such as meal or crumbled biscuit in a little warm milk, plus just a small amount of

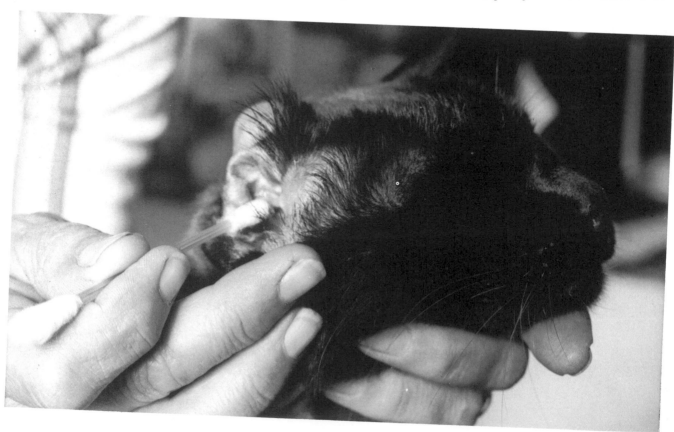

chopped raw meat. Anti-diarrhoea tablets are available, but if you can manage without them all the better. The last thing you want to do is to bind the patient up. If diarrhoea persists for more than two or three days, please gttv—there could be something seriously wrong inside.

Longhaired cats tend to suffer from hairballs. The cat grooms itself, hairs get on to the tongue and are swallowed. They then mass together into an indigestible solid ball which has to be excreted, often with great difficulty. Fortunately many cats seem to have foreknowledge of what can occur, and they eat grass as an emetic or otherwise contrive to throw up the hairball before it gets troublesome. But the only really safe solution is for the owner to brush his or her longhaired cat daily, with special care when he's moulting, so there are fewer hairs available to swallow. Regular grooming becomes a habit, and needn't take more than a few minutes each day.

No one but the vet can cope with a broken bone, but there could be occasions when knowledge of basic First Aid for fractures would come in handy. For instance, if your cat got his tail caught in a slamming door it would almost certainly break. The best thing to do would be to arrange some sort of splint to keep the tail straight and reasonably immobile, then hightail (if you'll forgive the expression) it to the vet. Same goes for obviously broken limbs. All fractures should be disturbed as little as possible,

Left: Make sure you follow the vet's instructions on care for ear infections.
Right: This is no joke to Puss! She is short-sighted and has been prescribed her very own pair of (non-National-Health) glasses!

and the patient should be kept very warm on the way to the vet's surgery, for fear of shock developing. A heavy rug wrapped around the cat will help to keep it still and will protect your hands, as also will a pair of thick leather gloves—even the best of friends may scratch when frightened and in pain.

One form of sickness in cats is quite literally just that: gastritis, of which the symptoms are sickness, thirst and refusal to eat. This is not serious unless it's accompanied by a high temperature, but if the cat's temperature does rise, you could have a case of feline gastro-enteritis on your hands and that could be a killer. So the vet is needed at once. However, simple gastritis—usually due to a chill or to eating something unsuitable—as a rule responds to a dose of mild laxative, a day's fast then a gradual return to normal diet via light things such as beef tea, finely minced lean meat, and milk.

Nowadays there are quite a lot of poisons about in house, gardens and fields. Most of them a cat wouldn't touch, but it's just possible that he/ she could accidentally ingest something harmful and become drowsy, with vomiting or diarrhoea, typical symptoms of poisoning. If you suspect that your cat is poisoned, get him to the vet *at once*—delay could be fatal. If you can, give him an emetic such as salt and water (1 in 4 teaspoons) before you leave.

In summertime cats, like people, sometimes suffer stings from wasps and bees—usually through their own fault because they try to catch the insects and play with them! The most likely place for a cat to be stung is on the front paw pads, and the best treatment is to swab the place with a fairly mild solution of bicarb in water, then to dry it and apply an anti-histamine cream.

Follow this with a lecture to puss on not catching any more wasps in future.

Those are some of the minor ills. Major ones include abscesses of all kinds, serious wounds with arterial bleeding or deep punctures, inflammation of the bowels, bronchitis, bad burns, feline distemper, infectious feline enteritis, the previously mentioned fractures and broken bones, pneumonia and any sort of tumour. All of these require professional diagnosis and treatment. Though with luck—and plenty of loving care—your cat may avoid them all for the whole of his long and happy life.

But the Grim Reaper comes to us all in the end, cats and humans alike . . . So if one day your cat goes off his food—not capriciously which you'd recognise because it would involve picking and choosing but seriously, with no interest at all in eating even if you tempt him over a period of days with all his favourite dishes—fear the worst. Consult your vet by all means, as you would for any serious disorder, but cats do seem to have built-in premonition where approaching death is concerned and when they reckon their time has come they just decide not to eat any more.

Felix, a big black and white neutered tom, was our friend for over twelve years. He'd led a rumbustious life and was a tough, self-sufficient fellow so we were rather surprised when he took to meeting us on the doorstep every evening when we came home from work; he also seemed to be getting less adventurous, more demonstrative and affectionate than ever before. We were glad later that we made a special fuss of him, in return. Then one day he refused food, and the same the next day and the next.

He spent most of his time on his favourite chair, not exactly sleeping but dozing a little and not paying much attention even to his mother who also lived with us and to whom he was devoted. On the third evening we rang the vet, who said 'Don't disturb him. I'll call on my way home.' He examined an unresisting Felix and gave his unwelcome verdict: a tired heart, a leaky valve, almost certainly the end. But it wasn't quite, not at least for two more weeks. Because the vet had said that there was no pain, just a tired feeling, we didn't feel we ought to rob Felix of his natural end by having him 'put down'. 'Just let him rest,' the vet advised. So we put his basket in the most comfortable place, where he could see us all and everyone could spare time to talk to him, and he took to it as an elderly person to their bed. At first he got out occasionally, to use his litter box or take a drink of water, but latterly there was no need for the box because he took no nourishment at all, and though we continued to offer invalid food all he would accept was a moistening of water on his parched tongue at frequent intervals. His big yellow eyes were often open in those last days, and a weak paw was sometimes stretched out to whoever was sitting with him; an almost imperceptible purr could still be heard if you put your head close to his. He knew he was going, and he'd made up his mind—I'm sure he had—to die with dignity, clean and comfortable, among his friends. And so he did. Dear Felix.

Right: 'I'm sure I've got anorexia: every time I look in the mirror I think I'm fat!' (Moral: a fat cat may be a jolly cat—but unless well advanced in years, he is not usually a healthy one)

Hungry Cats

Nobody actually says that it's time for breakfast or supper. Nobody makes a sound—they wouldn't be so undignified. But if you happen to go into the kitchen at (say) 0730 or 1800 hours, there they are—one on a chair, one on the windowsill—and they've both got their eyes on you. Just looking, of course. So you check your watch. Yes, they're right: it's time for breakfast. Or supper, as the case may be. Cats are always right.

Originally cats fed entirely off meat or fish, probably only just dead and dripping gore, for in those days they were mighty hunters. And as anyone with a garden knows, their tamed descendants are still capable of catching the odd mouse, vole or bird. (Some cats are kind enough to offer such small game to their owners, as loving tribute!). But today cat cuisine is a human responsibility—so how best to discharge it acceptably, healthily, economically?

Meat and fish are still favourite and essential foods, and one or other should be given to your cat daily. But cereals and cooked vegetables can help to provide a wider range of vitamins and minerals as well as valuable bulk, so it's worth offering small quantities of these together.

Probably one of the most famous cats in advertising. Though some years have passed since his death, Arthur is still a well-remembered star

What sort of meat and fish, and how much?

Offal, rabbit, chicken, horsemeat will all do, but all these should be cooked first. So should all kinds of fish (some cats like one fish more than another, but as a general rule all varieties are acceptable). Beef or lamb (fairly lean bits, cats aren't keen on fat unless it's well-crisped bacon rind) can be given either cooked or raw. Liver shouldn't be given more than once a week, so experts say. An adult cat needs 5 to 6 oz (approximately between 140 and 170 grams) of meat or 7 to 8 oz (200–225 g) fish daily, divided between two meals. So really an ideal day's menu could consist of 3 to 4 oz (about 85 to 110 g) fish, cooked and flaked and accompanied by a small spoonful of chopped cooked cabbage, spinach or carrot, for breakfast; then in the evening 2 or 3 oz (about 55 to 85 g) minced beef either raw or cooked, with a little crunchy meal or a biscuit or two on the side. Plus a saucer of milk after each meal if he likes it, and plenty of fresh water always available.

Sounds like a five star cat restaurant—counsel of purrfection —quite a lot of trouble—quite expensive?

Well I did say that it was an ideal

menu, and most of us realise that we can't always catch up with our ideals. But you do want your cat to have the best you can give him, don't you? And it's not much trouble really, if you plan ahead. For instance, the breakfast vegetable can be saved from a family meal the previous day and kept fresh in the fridge overnight (but please take it out in good time because cats don't care for very cold food). And the meal and biscuits are bought ready-made from any pet shop.

As for expense, if you allow for 6 oz meat (about 170 g) a day for four days that means about 1½ lb (about 680 g) of cheap cuts a week. Plus 8 oz fish (about 225 g) daily for three days (not 'cat bits' unless the budget is very tight because they're mostly bone, fin and skin), then you're going to spend between £2 and £3 a week, depending on where you shop and what you buy. Which is a lot to some people and not such a lot to others. What *everyone* should do, really, is think carefully before taking on a pet—and if they can't afford it, then don't. But for someone who lives alone, and wants the company of a cat (or dog, or budgie) can give, then the money is well spent. Also, I've heard of cats which share their owners' diets, and do very well—but this really does have to be started in kittenhood.

It's much put about that to feed your cat(s) on tinned or dried or packet food is lazy, irresponsible or even cruel; that if you decide to take a cat into your home you should also take the trouble to prepare fresh food for it every day and by not doing so you could cause serious injury to its health.

I don't agree. Nowadays pet foods are manufactured from strictly monitored ingredients under completely hygienic conditions. What goes into each tin is a well-balanced mixture which usually contains added vitamins and minerals for extra health and vitality. It's just possible that if he ate out of tins and packets all the time your pet could enjoy a more balanced diet, richer in vitamins and minerals, than you do! But if you are going to give him these 'convenience' foods, there are a few things to remember.

Tinned food is mushy, so what's he going to sharpen and clean his teeth on? Make sure he has a crisp titbit or two, to nibble every day—dried meat as sold by the pound in some pet shops, crisp bacon rind, a spoonful of puppy meal maybe.

Some cats like crunching a plain (human food) biscuit, and that's good for teeth and gums too provided it isn't a sweet one (try a piece of water biscuit or cream cracker); some—especially if living with the same family as a dog—enjoy gnawing a modest bone.

Most packet foods are dry. Lots of cats love them dearly, but concerned owners will make sure that they follow the manufacturer's instructions and leave plenty of fresh clean water easily available for drinking before, during and after meals.

Cats like variety: they tend to get tired of their favourite tin or packet; when that happens it's a sign that you should have changed it—yesterday at the latest! Cats are fussy eaters; if they take against a particular food they're quite cap-

Learning to share is part of growing up!

able of starving themselves. They'll waste both the food and their owner's money, by leaving what's put on their plate to go bad day after day until something different is produced, I know cats which know about colours—yes, honestly! —and will come-and-get-it eagerly if the tin about to be opened is red, but turn aside and leave the room with nose in air if it's green (vice versa if the red tin is produced more than three times running!).

Seriously, convenience foods for pets are not harmful, and for house-bound and handicapped owners they can be indispensable. But you wouldn't want to get your own food out of tins or packets *every* day of life, would you? And that's one good reason for making sure, if it's within your capacity, that your cat doesn't either.

Ours eat twice a day, as pre-scribed: breakfast and supper. They usually scoff what's put on their plates fairly quickly, with good appetite and good manners (no pushing, no pinching from the other plate), but if anything's left over we put a cover over it and half an hour later someone will probably come wandering back into the kitchen and look around as if to say 'I'm sure I left some of my breakfast somewhere', in which case we whip off the cover and madam tucks in again. Any food left after that gets put out on the (too high for cats) bird table, much to the delight of thrushes, starlings and blackbirds.

They loathe being given the same for breakfast as they had for supper last night, even if it's an all-time

Training a cat to 'beg', 'catch' or 'play ball' treads dangerous ground between the cute and the clever. All the same, the touch of a gentle paw from a hungry cat can work wonders

favourite like sprats. So we buy small quantities at a time: half a pound (about 225 g) of sprats makes a good meal for the two of them, provided I crumble a little brown bread on to each plate as well and then pour the liquor the fish were cooked in over all; they lap that up first, before setting about the delicate task of de-boning the sprats. I never take bones out for them, even from bigger pieces of fish. I know that this is contrary to all the rules but we've never had a choking accident yet and they seem to enjoy doing it for themselves, also the care they have to take makes them eat more slowly which surely must be good for digestion. Perhaps if they were big greedy tom cats instead of neat well brought up (not so young any longer), ladies, and liable to bolt their food, I might do some filleting.

It's very important indeed to keep a cat's feeding bowl or plate clean. It should be washed up after every meal, just as you wash your own plates. This is not just for obvious reasons of hygiene but because cats are such fastidious creatures and can actually be put off their food if it is given to them on a dirty plate. Some people disapprove of washing a cat's plate in the bowl used for the family washing up. If so, there's no harm—except slight extra work and more hot water—in keeping them separate. I don't, because I don't believe that cats are dirtier than humans (I'm not convinced really that it isn't the other way round!). But I do make sure that the plates are well scraped before putting them into the water, and if serving tinned food I wash them last, or in separate water, to be sure of avoiding any residual smell.

It's important too to change drinking water at least once a day, maybe twice in hot weather.

What about milk, the trad drink for cats? Ours don't drink it at all, never have since they were weaned. Possibly because Maude comes from tough Bermondsey stock which has never known the plush life and never got the taste for cow's milk, so she never liked it or taught her children to like it. But very occasionally, as a special treat, they do enjoy a spoonful of cream—this started when I left an almost empty small carton on top of the fridge one day, turned my back for a second and when I turned round found mother Maude, looking surprised but smug, licking cream off her whiskers. Yes I know it's a wicked indulgence, but everyone, cats included, feels better for a treat now and again.

When a cat is pregnant, her appetite is likely to increase and (in our experience at any rate) almost double again during lactation. After all, to begin with she's eating for three or four new lives growing inside her, and later on running an ever-open milk bar for hungry youngsters. She may appreciate the extra food she needs not in the form of more on her plate at her usual mealtimes but as another meal or two during the course of the day—lunch and tea, perhaps, as well as breakfast and supper. Most cats are very sensible about not over-eating, so there's little need to worry about that. Give as much as she asks for, and if she leaves any on her plate just remove it. You'll soon be able to judge how much she really needs.

Whether or not a cat is usually a milk drinker, during pregnancy and lactation her health will benefit if she can be persuaded to take a saucer of milk or a proprietary milky drink such as Lactol once or twice a day. Lactol, which contains essential vitamins, proteins, fats, casein and albumen, is also good for baby kittens if their mother has difficulty in feeding a big litter. But as a general rule a healthy cat has no trouble in nursing her family, so it isn't until they are four or five weeks old that they begin to need food other than that which she provides for them from her own body.

When it's time for weaning to begin they should be offered tiny quantities of scraped raw meat or flaked cooked fish, plus a little Lactol or warmed cow's milk. By the time they are eight weeks old they should be eating four meals a day, to include finely minced fresh meat or fish, minced cooked vegetables (now's the time to get them used to the taste), an occasional raw egg well beaten and either mixed with the other food or given in milk, special kitten meal from the pet shop and/or finely crumbled wholemeal bread. Do remember that the amounts should be really small, perhaps a teaspoon or two to begin with for each kitten, and do watch throughout the meal to make sure that each one gets its share.

The four meals a day programme can be reduced to three larger ones at about four months, and at seven months, bingo, a kitten becomes an adult cat and needs only two meals a day, which is where we came in.

If a cat is ill, he'll become even more choosy about his food. According to his illness, you may decide, or be advised by the vet, to fast him for a day or two or to tempt his appetite and try to build up his strength. If the latter, it's a question of small portions of his favourite foods, finely cut up and put on his plate as usual. Or if he can't manage solids, juiced or jellied

Above: 'If I hide up here, they're bound *to remember my food when they get their own.' Below right: This lucky puss is home-testing cat food*

and offered on a spoon. If he really seems to loathe the sight of all food, offer Lactol; and if that fails too, try to get him to drink some fresh water. One book in my cat library suggests that a few drops of gin, placed on a cat's tongue, often acts as an appetiser! I haven't yet had to resort to such an extreme, but can't help thinking that neat gin would be much too strong. Maybe the cat's owner should drink it, and so fortify him/herself to cope with the worry of having a sick furry friend! If complete refusal of food persists for three or four days or more, the vet should be consulted without further delay.

Special Cat Treats
(Some of these involve eating between meals, so should be strictly limited.)

● Being allowed to lick the top of a carton of cream when a layer of the thick yummy stuff is clinging to it. This tastes best of all to a cat which thinks it has outwitted its owner, so don't let yours realise that you left the top lying on the kitchen table on purpose.

● Just one raw sprat quickly filched from the bag before it's tipped into the saucepan with all the others and cooked properly for supper.

● A few trimmings when somebody's cutting up meat for a stew or paté, provided the cook realises that a cat appreciates having a little lean meat left on the gristle, chops

the trimmings finely and is prepared to let her friend sit at her elbow and watch the whole process.

● Chicken livers are good if they're just plain stewed or grilled, but specially delicious if they're washed, lightly seasoned, tossed in butter then covered and allowed to simmer very gently for ten to fifteen minutes, stirring occasionally. No reason why a cat's owner shouldn't eat the lot for his/her own supper, on a crisp round of toast; but a cat which knows it's much-loved can usually wheedle a share simply by sitting and watching the cooking process, and drooling (yes, some cats do). Not more than 3 oz (about 85 g) at a time per cat, because they're very rich, and only once a week at the most. The livers should be chopped before being served, to prevent greedy cats from swallowing them whole.

● Smoked Mackerel Mousse: a luxury really, even though it's quite cheap to make. Most cats will be delighted enough to be given mackerel cooked or mackerel smoked, so why take the trouble to mess around with a mousse? Because you love to please your pet, that's why! Anyhow . . . take 4 oz (or about 110 g) smoked mackerel, weighed after boning and filleting (supermarkets sell it even if your fishmonger doesn't) and break into small pieces. Now blend it, either in an electric blender or by rubbing through a sieve, with 1 oz (about 30 g) butter (margarine is cheaper, naturally, and works just as well, but cats *prefer* butter), add a few drops of lemon juice and a pinch of pepper. And if yours is an elderly gourmet and a very pampered cat, half a teaspoon of cooking brandy. Mix all well together, transfer to a couple of shallow glass jars or ramekins, and seal with melted butter. If kept in the fridge this will last for several days and be greatly appreciated as a very special delicacy (serve only about a teaspoon at a time). Humans enjoy it too, with toast or thin brown bread, and it stores well in the deep freeze.

● Buffy Butter. This treat, as far as I know, relates to only one special cat, our Buffy. But where she leads no doubt others could follow if they were encouraged to do so. Early on in life Buffy developed this habit of jumping on to the kitchen windowsill during breakfast and from there staring hard at something on the table. We finally realised that what she was looking at was the butter, and it wasn't long before the penny dropped and we realised why: she didn't see why she shouldn't have some if everyone else was. Someone of course was weak enough to give in, and . . . But because Buffy is a self-controlled cat, and not too greedy, she doesn't often ask for it (which is a good thing, or she would surely be the most cholesterolised—if there *is* such a word—cat in the country), but when she does it's routine for someone to cut off just a small piece of the delicious yellow stuff and put it on the palm of their hand. Buffy then transfers from the windowsill to that person's knee and very slowly, very delicately and with great relish licks the butter until it has all gone, licks the favoured hand which has fed her until it is clean and dry, jumps down on to the floor and gives her whiskers a good wash. When she has finished that she strolls across to the back door and stares at it—just as she stared at the butter—and behold it opens for her at once. One of her humans is always at hand to fulfil her every wish. After all, what else are humans for?

Tail piece

We occasionally have visiting cats in the house, left here while their owners are away from home in some emergency. When it happens our own are polite (though sometimes a bit sulky, like turning the back when spoken to), and very rarely hostile, though that too *has* been known to happen. But mealtimes used to be a problem. It seemed so inhospitable to feed one's own cats in the warm kitchen and put the visitor(s) outside or in another room (anyhow the latter would be seen by ours as a privilege, and therefore favouritism). So everybody had to eat at once, and in the kitchen. But often they just wouldn't—the air was thick with suspicion and nobody touched a morsel.

Fortunately that's all in the past. We've learned to dish out the food equally, each cat's meal on his/her own plate, and put the plates down in a row at intervals of about two feet (a little over $\frac{1}{2}$ metre). Cats are then called. They come, and investigate the food. Each in turn is named, and gently stroked from shoulders to tip of tail once or twice. For some reason known only to cats this is pleasing and soothing. It results in a row of contented eaters, up tails all. And if anybody hesitates for a moment in mid-meal, another stroke and a word of praise set her off again, until her plate is empty.

Travelling Cats

reatures of habit, sometimes more attached to places than to people, cats much prefer a stay-at-home life. Certainly they like to patrol their own territory. If they're so lucky as to live in the country, that may be quite far and wide. But in their opinion that's not travelling, that's just going walkabout; they do it when they feel like it, and come back indoors when the mood takes them—they're in control.

So what do you suppose a cat thinks when he/she is suddenly taken on a journey to somewhere he doesn't know, doesn't care about and would much rather never see? I say suddenly, because however much you try to give advance warning the actual pick-up and put-in-a-basket and take-in-the-car must appear sudden unless you do the putting in a basket well ahead of time. This may be a necessary precaution with the intuitive cat, who may easily guess that something's up and quietly disappear. On the other hand it may be just an added strain, if your cat's going to have to sit there and cry for an hour or more before you get the car out.

A few cats are of placid nature, and patient, and so devoted to and trusting in their owners that they

make no fuss at all about travelling. If yours is one of these, be thankful —and you deserve to be a little proud too, of having earned such devotion. Cats of this disposition are obviously well-suited for showing, too, because journeys from home to show and back cause them little stress; though if shown regularly cats do manage to get accustomed to travelling. Some may even begin to enjoy it as part of their routine.

If a cat absolutely *has* to travel, far the best way for him/her to do so is with his owner, in a car, possibly accompanied by a second person whom the cat knows and trusts. The companion will do for extra company and for soothing the cat if he becomes panicky and tries to get out of his basket.

However much under control a cat may appear to be, I'd never

Left: Some sort of receptacle is essential for taking your cat away from home—even if only to the local vet. He'll appreciate it all the more when other locals (dogs, boa constrictors?) start a rucus-while-you-wait. Right: The law requires human beings to wear belts, and cats too need some kind of safety restraint. This passenger may look comfortable, but he would be safer attached to a lead or harness

74

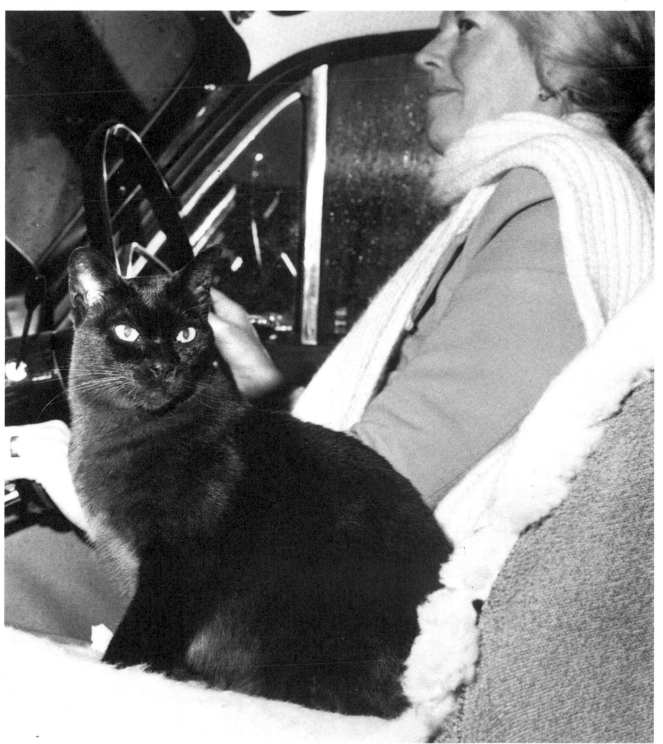

advise taking one on a journey, or even out to the car, without putting him in his basket first (and making sure he can't get out of it, too!), because you just can't be certain that he won't try to escape at the last minute, jumping out of your arms and possibly even scratching you in the process, whether he means to or not. Also you can't be sure of what he'd do if there were some sort of crisis en route—for example if there was an accident, or even if you just had to stop very quickly, he might end up on your knee or under your feet. That would be no joke if you were trying to concentrate on your driving!

Again, say you had to get out yourself for some reason, or your passenger did, he might be tempted to make a run for it while the door was open and, panicked by traffic, rush away and get lost or worse still be knocked down and injured. He might even decide to jump out of a too far open window!

Such grisly possibilities! So however clever cats may look sitting on the parcel shelf at the back of a car (especially on the continent where it seems to me I see lots of them doing it) and watching the scenery go by, please don't let yours do that. French and German cats often wear collars, and may therefore be attached to a lead which someone in the car may be holding, and this of course would be a sensible precaution, but even so I don't think it's the safest way to travel.

The next best thing is to go by bus, provided you can keep cat-in-basket on your knee—which means,

A walk on the safe side: training a cat to a lead can be time-consuming, but it proves its worth when he is able to accompany you on rambles instead of being left behind pining

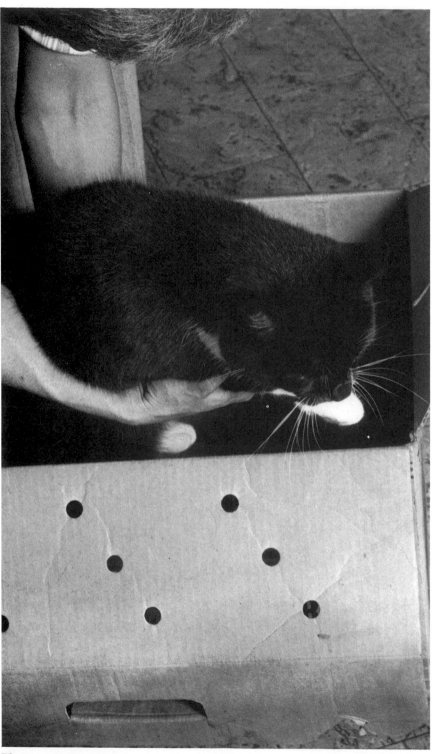

for a start, avoiding rush hour travel. But that's not always practicable or permitted. On a train—if you're taking only one cat—he can probably travel with you, but if you have several they'll have to go in the guard's van. The cat's journey will have to be paid for, the charge depending on the weight of the cat plus basket, and the distance to be travelled.

The worst way to travel, from a cat's point of view, must surely be by plane or boat, unaccompanied. Fortunately this doesn't often have to happen, but when it does the cat's owner can make it a little easier for him by accustoming him to his travelling box (in those circumstances a basket wouldn't be suitable) during the previous week or two—putting him into it at first for a short time then gradually for longer periods, reassuring him when he goes into it, making a big fuss of him when he's taken out; the important thing being to demonstrate to him that he does always get out after a time, and that someone will be there to greet him and praise him for being so patient and brave.

What sort of container/box/ basket is best for a travelling cat? Ours travel by car, if ever they have to, and each has her own cat basket, the wicker sort with a flat floor, straight sides and curved roof. One end is wicker all-in-one with the rest, but the other has a removable 'door' of strong criss-cross wire which can be tightly fixed to the basket by five leather straps—two at each side and one at the top. (It's

A purpose-built box of strong cardboard, with plenty of airholes, feels secure and gives privacy; but a travelling pen from which puss can see the world may be best from his point of view —he likes to know where he's going, after all!

not necessary to unfasten all five every time. The two at one side can be left permanently done up and used as hinges, provided you always check before each journey to make sure that they haven't come loose.) There's also a leather handle in the top of the basket, by which it can be carried. This sort of basket is comfortable (as long as you put a cushion or twice-folded rug or piece of towelling on the floor), friendly (travelling companions can put a finger through the wire mesh door to stroke a cat's head and reassure him, also the cat can see out so he knows where he's going and who he's with), and impossible to escape from; you can buy them at most good pet shops. Their only drawback is that they can be draughty—not a problem in a car but if you're taking your cat by bus or rail he'd probably prefer it, and be less likely to catch cold, if you lined the basket about halfway up with thick material inside or wrapped it round with stout paper outside (being careful of course not to exclude all ventilation).

A cat which is to travel unaccompanied, or to be put in the guard's van during the journey, would probably be better off in a wooden box (not too heavy to lift, though) or a purpose-made fibre-glass container such as also can be bought in pet shops. He's probably going to hate the journey anyhow, and it will pass more quickly for him, and be less frightening, if he can curl up in semi-darkness without any outside distractions and go to sleep. Provide a folded piece of blanket

An example of a stout, wired-netted cat pen. These two friends seem to be sharing it amicably enough. In fact, many owners who have two cats find that they do like to travel together—it saves you room and it gives them someone to talk to!

for him to lie on, or wood shavings —never hay or straw because it's sneezy and itchy and may contain ticks. Make sure that the container has a handle on top, proper ventilation holes, and the words LIVE CAT printed very large on top and on every side. I would also put THIS WAY UP PLEASE, with suitable arrows, but maybe I'm over-fussy.

Airlines and steamship companies have their own regulations about travelling cats and other animals. You should contact the one you intend to use in good time before the journey, and make sure that you comply with all the rules—if not, your pet's journey could be delayed at the last minute or even interrupted halfway. Usually a special box container is insisted on, with receptacles for food and water, and a litter box.

Unless you know for certain that your cat is a good traveller, don't feed him before a journey. Throwing up is such a messy business, distressing for both him and you, and stopping to clean out a box or basket can be complicated if not impossible. It won't harm him to fast for a few hours and he'll enjoy a good meal all the more when you arrive at your destination. Owners of show cats seldom feed them on the morning of the show, just giving them supper when they get back home.

Cats can catch and/or carry rabies, so in common with a number of other animals they are subject to quarantine regulations—which is a very good reason for not even beginning to consider taking your cat with you on a holiday abroad. If you've been living abroad, and intend to bring a pet cat back to the UK, or if you want to import a pedigree cat from another country,

then you have to obtain a licence from the Ministry of Agriculture, Fisheries and Food, which will require the cat to spend six months, starting from the moment of disembarkation, in an approved cattery, and to be vaccinated. Further details of the regulations can be obtained from the Ministry at Whitehall Place, London, or from

its local offices (look in the phone book for the address). The RSPCA have a leaflet 'Sickness and Fright in Dogs and Cats Travelling by Train, Car or Airplane' which gives helpful advice too.

Some people take their cats on holiday with them in the UK, and I agree that this can be better than leaving them behind in a strange cattery (though if all goes well it won't continue to be strange and the cat may even approve of it warmly and in time learn to look upon it as a second home), but I still think that it is kinder to find a reliable person to come and live in your house and look after your pet(s) while you're away.

However the people who take their cats with them maintain that the animals prefer it to being left behind, and if you think as they do there's no harm in trying it. But do make sure that wherever you're going is ready to receive your cat as well as you. Is the house/hotel as cat-proof as your own home, with no unexpected openings to attics or cellars which a frightened cat could crawl into and get stuck or lost? Is the garden reasonably safe, with no busy road and confusing, dangerous traffic roaring by? Is it a clean environment, unlikely to harbour germs which he's unused to and might pick up? (this arises most frequently in the case of farm holidays). And are you sure that there is no other cat at the other end whose territory yours would be invading, thus causing stress to both of them? Is there a dog, or are there dogs, which might chase and terrify him? Do at least have a brood over all this before making plans.

Right: Who needs flunkeys to open doors for them? Ingenious cats will find their own way . . .

80

Top Cats

Suppose your cat isn't just a moggy-around-the-house but an aristocrat with a long pedigree. Suppose you bought him/her as a kind of hobby as well as a companion, and you have time and are willing to take trouble and spend money in the hope of making him a champion. What is the way to go about it?

Until about a hundred and twelve years ago comparatively few people were interested in the different breeds of cats which might exist, and pedigree breeds as known today weren't even established. But in 1871, due to the enthusiasm and determination of a Mr. Harrison Weir, who was not only a cat lover but an artist and a Fellow of the Horticultural Society (so had a good idea of the value of shows in promoting breeds and raising standards), the first Cat Exhibition took place at the Crystal Palace and was a huge success. It didn't take long for cat shows to become fashionable, especially as Queen Victoria owned a pair of Blue Persians and took an interest in what was developing. In 1887 the National Cat Club was formed, and in 1910 the Governing Council of the Cat Fancy came into being.

Some good things not only en-dure but go from strength to strength! It is to the Governing Council of the Cat Fancy offices, now at 4 Penel Orlieu, Bridgwater, Somerset, that owners still write for information and a copy of the Rules of the Fancy; and all pedigree kittens must be registered with the Governing Council before they can be shown—the Council is the official registering body in the UK, and also grants the licences for shows, awards certificates and approves judges.

Having registered your kitten, loved and cherished him, fed him sensibly and groomed him regularly, the time comes to decide when and where you want to show him, so you write to the Fancy for a list of shows (enclosing s.a.e. please). You'll probably decide to try one or two small ones first, to see how your cat stands up to this new experience, and also it's sensible to get him used to being in a show pen by keeping him confined for an hour or two a day at home in a similar pen so that there'll be less danger of him doing a wild-tiger-

Left: There are correct ways to hold a cat, one demonstrated here by a judge at a cat show. Right: Being tops can be a bit of a yawn . . .

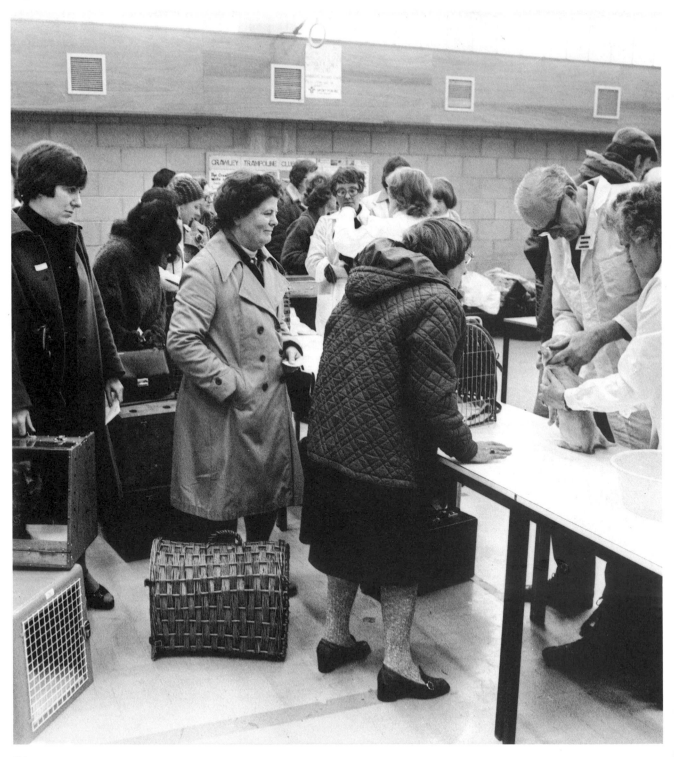

trying-to-get-out act on the great day.

It's important to write to the manager of the show you want to enter as early as possible before the event: three months ahead is just about right. The manager will send a schedule of classes and an entry form, and after studying the schedule carefully to see whether and where your cat may fit in you fill up the entry form and send it with the appropriate fee(s) back to the manager in good time before the closing date. All you have to do now is to wait until you receive

acknowledgement of your entry plus the essential 'vetting-in' card (all entries are checked by a vet before being admitted to a show) and meantime make sure that your cat is in peak condition.

Obviously regular grooming and correct diet since kittenhood are worth more than last minute beautification, but that does count too and some people even give their cats — usually pale coloured, longhaired ones — a bath a few days before the show, or a dry shampoo using baby talcum powder, a proprietary dry shampoo recommended for cats' coats, or fuller's earth. All these should be used sparingly and thoroughly brushed out. A double check on eyes, ears and claws should be done the day before the show, and of course, an extra careful grooming on the day.

As to the actual procedure at a show, what usually happens is that 'vetting-in' takes place in the morning; after that owners take their cats to the penning section and

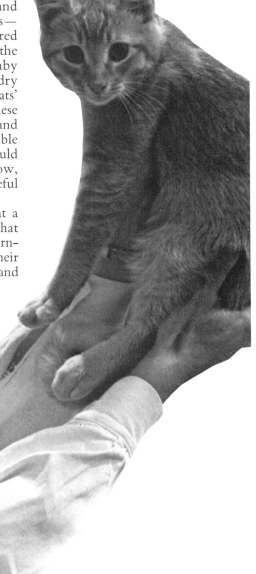

Left: Admission and 'vetting-in' for a show can take some time, so be prepared. It includes, of course, a brief physical inspection (below)

Right: Overview at a local cat show. Shows run the gamut, from Championship Events, through Exemption and Sanction Shows, which are especially valuable for newcomers, to local fairs where personality is the main key to a blue ribbon. Possibly most famous of all is the National Cat Club Show, held in London at the beginning of December every year

settle them down. Cats may not be sent to shows unaccompanied; they must be brought by their owner or owner's nominee, and they must travel in a proper cat basket or container; the owner or his/her nominee must be close at hand throughout the show, except when the hall is closed for judging.

Each cat has his own numbered pen into which he is expected to settle without fuss (this is where getting him used to a similar pen at home pays dividends), and must be provided with a sanitary tray and a clean white blanket without distinctive markings; if extra heat from a hot water bottle is thought to be necessary the bottle must be concealed beneath the blanket; any food or water container must be removed before judging begins (but many owners believe it best not to feed a cat at all before or during a show). A cat may be groomed with brush or comb or cloth immediately before penning, but no powder or other grooming aid may be used in the show hall.

Each judge is accompanied during the judging by a steward whose job it is to take each cat in turn from its pen and put it on a wheeled table or trolley for the judge to assess. If a cat behaves in such a way that it is unable to be handled by the steward it can be disqualified; if a cat bites a steward or a judge it will be reported to the manager of the show, and if it bites at three shows (heaven forbid!) it will be disqualified from all future shows. These are just some of the most important rules—for a full list you should write to the Governing Council of the Cat Fancy, enclosing s.a.e. and the fee which as I write this is £1.

So now to the great moment. The judges have examined all the exhibits, awarded prizes and made comments . . . Is your cat going to the top of the class? Show Rules of the GCCF state that championship shows in Britain have set classes—Cats Class for exhibits nine-months old or over on the day of the show, Kittens Class for exhibits of three to nine months; Neuters Class, Novice Class, and so on. The title of Champion for cats and Premier for neuters shall be granted to exhibits winning three Challenge Certificates at three shows under separate judges, and a GCCF Challenge Certificate will be offered for each Cat/Neuter Open Class of recognised breed with Championship status. Furthermore the title of Grand Champion will be granted to a cat winning three Champion Challenge Certificates at three shows under three separate judges, and similarly for neuters except that the title is Grand Premier. So you see there's plenty to go for!

Almost certainly the biggest and most exciting UK show is the National Cat Club Show which is held at Olympia in London each year on a Saturday early in December. The organiser, Grace Pond, FZS, is a distinguished judge of cats much in demand worldwide (when I telephoned to check the date of this year's Show, which will probably be 10th December, she had just got back from judging in Paris and was off to Dublin the next weekend). She is the author or editor of no less than twenty-four books about cats, and is justifiably delighted and proud that during the thirty years she has been running the Show the number of entries has increased from around 300 at first to over 2,000 now!

With such huge numbers of exhibits this is a tremendously interesting event to visit, even if you haven't a cat of your own which you wish to show. You can wander around the penning sections all day, get a proper idea of what the representatives of each breed look like, even talk to breeders—if they can spare the time—and find out more about each cat's characteristics. Also there are classes for pet cats as well as pedigree ones—I mean pet cats of uncertain pedigree—and this of course widens its scope and adds interest. And you may care to shop at the hundred or so stalls selling 'catty' goods. If you want to know more about the National Cat Club Show, write to The Organiser, Mrs. Grace Pond, at Greenhayes, 35 Blackwater Lane, Pound Hill, Crawley, Sussex; please enclose a stamped, self-addressed envelope. When a show's over, for winners and losers alike it's time to go home. So back into his basket with your favourite exhibit—and where on earth did we park the car? A good meal won't go amiss before bed, and a saucer of warm milk as a settler (maybe a drop of whisky in it—or in yours would be better—to celebrate?). If you have other cats, keep them separate from your champion-in-the-making for a week, just in case he's picked up any infection while away from home which he'd do better to keep to himself rather than spread around.

Well that wasn't too bad, was it? And the following day you'll probably be poring over the list of shows again, wondering which one to enter him for next!

Right: At a major show in Britain there may be between 1,000 and 2,000 pens. As the cats win prizes, cards are attached to their pens. 'Best in Show' takes place separately, after all the other prizes have been awarded

Heroic Cats

It's not easy for a cat to become a hero. Heroes are usually big and strong. Heroic dogs, for example, jump through windows and grab hold of clothing and drag a beloved human to safety; they stand over someone who is hurt and bark like mad until rescue comes. But whoever heard of a cat which could break a pane of glass, batter a door down, yell loud enough to attract attention?

Well yes, the last is possible. There's an idle great object called George who lives with his elderly lady friend in a south London suburb. They aren't well off and the social worker who keeps an eye on Mrs. X often used to wonder whether George wouldn't be better off in the Great Cat House in the Sky—his tins of food, his occasional fresh fish treat, his ointment for eczema and his packets of tonic tablets combined to make quite a big hole in the housekeeping money. Came the day when Mrs. X had a bad fall and couldn't move. She ran out of breath and strength to go on shouting for help. So it was George's voice which was still raised when the social worker came to the door and couldn't get in, George who squeezed his unwieldy bulk out of

Climbing in through a top storey window requires a certain degree of heroism. Knowing that you'll always land on your feet if you fall doesn't detract from the achievement either

an upstairs window and almost fell at her feet saying in cat language 'For Heaven's sake break in, something's very wrong, something's up!', George who persisted and led her round to the back and jumped up on a windowsill and showed her the kitchen window which was only just on the latch and could be opened from outside with an effort. George who saved a life, probably. So who says George isn't a hero?

Then again, there was Millie. Millie was unlucky enough to live in a house in a high risk flood area, and managed to combine this with motherhood in a most alarming way. What happened was that Millie's loving and caring owner prepared for her pregnant pet a splendid basket with *tout confort* which she decided to locate in her own bedroom. It was a light and airy place, but warm too, and nice and convenient should the happy event take place during the hours of darkness. This was their first pregnancy, needless to say, and Millie's owner hadn't heard what odd ideas mother cats sometimes have about maternity wards.

Then, in the middle of a dark and stormy night, there was a flood warning. Millie's owner got up and dressed. She searched everywhere, with increasing panic, for Millie who was not in her basket beside the bed. Eventually, under protest and much distressed, she was evacuated by the emergency services. Meanwhile Millie had been contentedly giving birth where she had always intended to give it—in the basement dining room where there happened to be a nice old sideboard with a cupboard door always ajar, all cosy and dark inside and just the right amount of space for a family. The only drawback was that now Millie and four newborn kittens were alone in the house and water was lapping two inches from the floor of the sideboard and still rising. No one knows how she did it, because no one else was there. But when they were found, two days later, the kittens were fine, and Millie was exhausted but not too bad, and all five of them were right on top of that old sideboard in a position which one would have thought impossible for Millie to reach on her own, let alone encumbered by kittens. In fact, kittens four times up and three journeys down—with flood water creeping ever higher (and you know how cats fear water). Yes, Millie was a heroine all right.

No doubt there have been many more of them, unidentified and uncelebrated, brave but obscure cat heroes and heroines. But in searching for famous ones I must confess I've had little luck. I did find a story about a cat who joined his owner in the Tower of London, helping to keep him alive by catching pigeons

'He heard the sound of Bow Bells' . . . Dick Whittington became a rich man and was thrice Lord Mayor of London. But this Victorian illustration isn't strictly accurate. At the time of the famous hearing, Dick's cat was in Africa earning his master a fortune by catching rats.

and bringing them in through the bars. It sounded a bit of a fantasy to me—most cats I know would have eaten the birds themselves! (Anyhow, how did they dispose of the feathers without the gaolers finding out what was going on?). And then there was Puss in Boots, the brave and resolute cat who helped his owner to become rich and marry a princess—but he only exists in fairy tale and pantomime.

There's a legend about the sacred cats of Burma which celebrates a hero. It tells how, many years ago, an old priest living in a temple in the mountains was attacked by robbers. The temple cat did its best to save the priest, but he was killed. As a reward for its bravery the goddess of the temple turned the rather ordinary looking white cat into a beautiful golden creature with huge blue eyes and a handsome seal-coloured head, ears and tail. Only its paws remained white, as a symbol of purity. Today, almost identical sacred cats, presumably descendants of that first heroic ancestor, are increasingly popular as distinguished looking pets in Europe and America.

I found a few cat heroes in a book about animals which saw action in wartime, but most of these, to my mind, don't really qualify. Heroism, surely, must be deliberate, and voluntary. If someone picks you up and adopts you as their mascot and takes you into action in their tank, ship or aeroplane there's nothing much you can do about it except endure, and you don't really qualify as a celebrated hero for that.

Left: Simon, the Navy's heroic cat, still lies buried at Ilford. But visitors to his plot are fewer today than in the 1950s when the original stories of his bravery caught the public imagination

The alternative might be to leap overboard or out, and become a famous coward! For most of the mascots this would not only have been impossible, but even more terrifying.

For some unknown reason a cat named Salty—mascot of the San Diego Coast Guard Air Station—once stowed away with her kittens on an amphibious reconnaissance plane and so took part in the rescue of a flier who had ditched in the ocean. But it had to be admitted later that her presence was due more to curiosity than to heroic instincts.

Closest to being a war hero, perhaps, and certainly celebrated as one, was Simon, a cat presented to the commanding officer of HMS *Amethyst* in Hongkong in 1948. He was enthusiastically adopted as a mascot by the ship's company. In spring of the following year the *Amethyst*, at sea off mainland China, was fired upon by shore-based batteries. One of the first shells wrecked the Captain's cabin, and Simon received minor wounds and burns. His first instinct was to hide, and lick his wounds in safety, but when he was called upon to undertake immediate rat-catching duties (the shelling had disturbed rodents in the bilges and they were now scavenging throughout the ship, a real danger to the crew's health), he fell to with alacrity and made a number of kills. For bravery and devotion to duty under shell fire Simon was recommended—with the consent and approval of his commanding officer—for the Dickin Medal, the animals' Victoria Cross, by the Allied Forces Mascot Club of the People's Dispensary for Sick Animals (the medal is named in memory of Mrs. M. E. Dickin, founder of the PDSA).

On returning to Hongkong a

huge post awaited Simon, with letters and presents from all over the world; and on the way home to Britain he was feted at every port of call. But sadly the story does not have a happy ending. He had, of course, to go into quarantine when the *Amethyst* reached the UK, and there he died just over three weeks later—whether weakened by after-effects of his wounds and so much strenuous rat catching, broken hearted at being parted from all his friends on board ship, or just worn out by so much praise and fuss no one will ever know.

However, he was buried with suitable honours at the PDSA cemetery at Ilford and a fine gravestone with the Dickin Medal and the badge of HMS *Amethyst* carved upon it was presented by an admiring firm of stonemasons. Another memorial, carved and presented by the sculptor Elizabeth Muntz, can be seen at the PDSA in Plymouth, *Amethyst*'s home port, where the Dickin Medal was presented posthumously a few months later.

Cats in Phrase and Fable

SAY CHESHIRE CHEESE

*Hey diddle diddle, The cat and the
  fiddle,
The cow jumped over the moon,
The little dog laughed to see such fun,
And the dish ran away with the
  spoon . . .*

For most children the cat in that old rhyme is one of the very first literary cats they hear about. But it's soon followed by the adventures of soft-hearted Orlando, the Marmalade Cat; by the enigmatic Cheshire Cat in Lewis Carroll's Alice in Wonderland, whose grin kept coming and going — one big grin he was, really; by Edward Lear's beautiful pussycat who went sailing with an amorous owl, danced by the light of the moon and eventually married the bird taking the ring at the end of a willing pig's nose as the symbol of their undying love; by Mrs. Tabitha Twitchit and her volatile family Tom Kitten (always tearing his trousers), Moppet and Mittens created by Beatrix Potter. What a fine, busy lot those literary cats were, to be sure, in nursery days!

But some eminent writers have taken a more realistic view. Chaucer, for instance — one of England's earliest poets — was one of the first to record the contrariness of cats:

*Lat take a cat, and fostre him well with
  milk
And tendre flessh, and make his couche
  of silk,
And lay hym seen a mous go by the
  wal,
Anon he weyveth milk and flessh and
  al,
And every deyntee that is in that hous,
Swich appetit hath he to ete a mous.*

(The Manciple's Tale)

Matthew Arnold, writing 'Poor Mathias', an elegy to his canary, over four hundred years later, saw cats not just as contrary-minded domestic creatures but as symbolising some of Man's harshest qualities:

*Cruel, but composed and bland,
Dumb, inscrutable and grand,
So Tiberius might have sat,
Had Tiberius been a cat.*

Montaigne, the great French philosopher, wondered in 1580:

*Quand je me joue a ma chatte, qui sait
si elle passe son temps de moi plus que
je ne fais d'elle? (When I play with
my cat, who knows whether she isn't
amusing herself with me more than I
am with her?)*

Doctor Johnson, mighty man of letters, is known to have deferred to at least one cat, considering its feelings most politely:

*'When I observed he was a fine cat,
saying "Why yes, Sir, but I have had
cats whom I liked better than this";
and then, as if perceiving Hodge to be
out of countenance, adding "but he is a
very fine cat, a very fine cat indeed".'*

Boswell further recorded that Doctor Johnson would go in person to buy oysters (yes, oysters! But we must remember that in those days they were the fodder of the poorer classes.) for Hodge, in case the servants should think it too much trouble and so take a dislike to his precious pet.

The poet Christopher Smart, 1722–71, wrote a definitely-on-the-side-of-cats tribute *To My Cat, Jeoffrey*. (This, incidentally, has been most enchantingly set to music by Ruth Gipps, conductor of the Chanticleer Orchestra and, until her retirement a year or two ago, a Professor at the Royal College of Music — hear it sometime if you possibly can):

*For when he takes his prey he plays
  with it to give it a chance.
For one mouse in seven escapes by his
  dallying . . .*

'I have often seen a cat without a grin—but a grin without a cat . . .' The wonderful cat of Lewis Carroll's Alice's Adventures in Wonderland *had a disconcerting habit of appearing and disappearing slowly, bit by bit. The original illustrations were by Sir John Tenniel*

For he keeps the Lord's watch in the night against the adversary.
For he counteracts the powers of darkness by his electrical skin and glaring eyes.
For he counteracts the Devil, who is death, by brisking about the life . . .
For he is the quickest to his mark of any creature.
For he is tenacious of his point.
For he is a mixture of gravity and waggery.
For he is good to think on, if a man would express himself neatly . . .

Quite some cat, Jeoffrey must have been! But certain people do seem to ask a lot of cats, though the nineteenth century essayist J. A. Froude was apparently in lighter mood when among his Short Studies on Great Subjects he wrote *The Cat's Pilgrimage* in which the cat was made to ask *What is my duty?* to which another animal replied *Get your own dinner!* but the Owl said *Meditate, O Cat!*

Legend has it that a little cat called Meuzza was the much-loved companion of the prophet Mohammed, and that one day when the call came to prayer Meuzza was sleeping in the prophet's robe. Mohammed cut off the sleeve on which the cat was sleeping, rather than disturb it. Later, Mohammed stroked Meuzza three times, thus ensuring him a place in Paradise; and he gave all cats freedom for ever from the fear of falling, by granting them the ability always to land on their feet.

In current times there have been many notable literary cats. All those celebrated by T. S. Eliot, for instance; so many great cat characters that it's difficult to choose which to pick out for special mention. My own favourites, both from *Old Possum's Book of Practical Cats*, are *Bustopher Jones: The Cat About Town* who dressed in impeccable black with white spats, patronised all the best clubs for delicious snacks of shrimps and venison, and in the course of time grew 'unmistakably round', and the elusive *Macavity, the Mystery Cat*, tall, thin, ginger-haired and outwardly respectable

95

T. S. Eliot's 'Old Possum's Book of Practical Cats' was made into a long-running, ecstatically-received musical, Cats, *which celebrated the exploits of a series of eccentric felines (including philosophers and amateur gangsters)*

but when a crime is committed:

*He's the bafflement of Scotland Yard,
the Flying Squad's despair,
For when they reach the scene of crime
—Macavity's not there!*

And have you ever met Flyball, Ruthven Todd's *Space Cat*, who wore an inflated suit with a special tail and accompanied Captain Fred Stone on flights to the moon and other planets? Flyball had a very nasty experience on Mars, when a metallic mouse decided to play with him instead of the usual vice versa; but he also managed to save Fred's life (and his own) through his great ingenuity in finding suitable sticky plants with which to patch their space helmets . . .

Jennie Baldwin, a stray tabby in Paul Gallico's *The Abandoned*, had a set of life-preserving rules which she taught to a boy called Peter Brown who had been turned into a cat. The first rule was *When in doubt, wash—because it feels so good to be clean.* And Tao, the Siamese cat in Sheila Burnford's *The Incredible Journey*, not only caught food as easily as his canine companions during their long trek through an inhospitable wilderness but also saved the bull terrier's life by holding a grown bear at bay and later reviving the unconscious dog with the smell of fresh meat.

*Left: A pull from a Victorian music sheet. Both the cat and the dog enjoyed a re-evaluation of their position in 19th-century society, climbing from a relationship of servant to man, to that of companion
Right: This illustration, from a 1909 edition of Kipling's Just So Stories, accompanied the tale 'The Cat That Walked By Himself'. The drawing was by the author.*

Another cat I can't resist is the splendidly naive and pompous William in James Thurber's *The Cat In The Lifeboat* (one of *Further Fables for Our Time*). William just knew that he must be the only cat in town called William; he convinced himself therefore that he was the Will of Last Will and Testament, and also the Willy of Willy Nilly. On a voyage around the world a storm arose and the ship began to sink. William was sure that somebody shouted: *William and children first!* so he jumped into a lifeboat, only to be thrown out immediately by an infuriated sailor. After a long swim he reached an island, where he survived; but life had lost its meaning because he could no longer remember who he was . . .

Cats have featured in some very funny films and comic strips (though cats themselves might not approve because the laughter is usually 'at' rather than 'with'). Remember Tom and Jerry in *Puss Gets The Boot* and *Cat Concerto*—they date back to 1939 and 1946 respectively, but must have been re-run many thousands of times and since 1965 many more cartoon films featuring Tom and Jerry have been made for MGM and featured on TV. Felix the Cat, a Chaplinesque loner who nevertheless was quick and resourceful and usually came out on top in the end, was one of the greatest characters ever in cartoon films; he first appeared in 1919 in *Feline Follies*, produced for Paramount by Pat Sullivan, and hundreds more films were made between then and 1933; in 1960 Felix was revived by

Left: Elinor Glyn with her two cats, Candide and Zandig (named after Voltaire's heroes), photographed by Paul Tanqueray, in 1931

Joe Orilo, who produced over 200 TV episodes about him. Felix even had a song written specially for him: *Felix Keeps On Walking*. Today in the US cartoonist Jim Davis's comic strip *Garfield*, about a fat cat with drooping eyelids and a lust for pasta, is syndicated nationwide and there have been three paperback bestsellers—*Garfield at Large*, *Garfield Gains Weight* and *Garfield Bigger Than Life*. Psychologists might work it out that this sort of thing is getting one back on cats for being so superior about the human race—who knows?

Back to books: there's an all-time cat classic which as far as I know is at present out of print but you might find it in a library. Called *The Tiger in the House*, and written in 1920 by Carl Van Vechten, it features, in its study of cat behaviour, a cat called Feathers which had no respect at all for Van Vechten's sleeping time but woke him up when she felt ready for breakfast in the morning by licking his cheek, nibbling his toes, walking all over him as he lay in bed. Feathers was adamantly jealous of other cats, understood a number of words, and liked to run up and down the piano keys at night, 'playing scales'!

No book about cats is complete without a mention of Dick Whittington's famous pet—which may or may not have existed in reality but its legend has certainly lived on. Poor Dick invested his only possession, a cat which he had bought for a penny to kill the mice in his attic room, in the enterprise of a rich merchant (well ahead of his time!), who believed that if his servants were given the opportunity to put in money it would bring him luck. The trading ship Unicorn, with Dick's cat on board, eventually reached the Barbary coast where

the cat rid a king's palace of rats and mice and in return the king paid a fortune for the cat and for the ship's cargo. Meantime Dick was slaving away in London; tired of working for a pittance he determined to seek his fortune elsewhere, but after hearing the encouraging message *Turn again Whittington, Lord Mayor of London* from Bow Bells he stuck to the job until the Unicorn returned and he received his share of the fortune. He then married his boss's daughter, went into trade and became even richer, and—guess what? —ended up as Lord Mayor. And believe it or not, there really was a Richard Whittington who was elected Lord Mayor three times, married a baronet's daughter and is remembered for his many gifts to charity. Whether he owned a cat as a boy—or not—is not recorded. But on top of the stone on Archway Road which stands to his memory, showing that his Mayoralties took place in the reigns of three separate monarchs—Richard II, Henry IV and Henry V—there stands guard a handsome cat.

Talking to Cats

*Y*ears ago, when we ran some extracts in SHE from a fascinating book called *How to Talk to Your Cat*, I came in for a certain amount of criticism from non-cat-lovers who reminded me that the median age of the magazine's readers was under thirty-five and added that in their opinion 'only old people talk to their cats'. As a confirmed talker to cats all my life, I couldn't agree. Why assume for a start that all elderly people are eccentric? They are most certainly not! And why think that only the old, eccentric and presumably lonely feel a need to confide in their four-footed friends? Arrogant nonsense that is, say I!

It is not in the least eccentric to get up in the morning and say 'Hello' to the cats. It's only polite. How would you like it if your cats came into the room and ignored you (though come to think of it if you don't talk to them they may easily do just that—because they'll have decided, sadly, that they're living with a superior sort of person who doesn't believe in communicating with cats, and they'll have given up trying). Most cat owners of necessity call their cats by name, saying things like 'Breakfast time, Tibbles', 'Supper's ready, Ginger',

'Come and get it, Tom', 'Grub up, Henrietta', and such. They can't very well open a door or window, either, without asking 'Do you want to go out, Mitzi?' or 'Coming in now, Chrysanthemum?' In fact on that simplistic level millions of people already *do* talk to their cats. But how many, I wonder, talk as freely as they would to their friends —and in return get a degree of love and companionship which would amaze the non-talkers?

Because our household is geared to cats, and our state of mind cat-orientated, no one thinks it odd to hear mother ask 'Coming upstairs? Well hurry then, I can't wait all day!' without getting any audible reply. No one tells me not to waste their time when I say 'Hang on a minute, I've forgotten to tell the cats we're going out. Must just say we won't be long.' That sort of thing is regarded as being among the essential courtesies which enrich the quality of cat/human relationships.

We tell our cats lots of things, and they always want to know. We speak softly in order not to alarm them—cats hate raised voices or indeed any loud noise—and they find it soothing and companionable. When good things happen for us,

they are pleased; if the opposite, they're sympathetic. If one of them is feeling cross, or nervous, or jealous of someone or some other cat, we stroke them and ask what the trouble is and tell them how much loved they are, and they soon begin to purr again. If one is ill, we talk about how brave they are and how kind and clever the vet is and how it-won't-hurt-much-more and they'll soon be better. While grooming them we tell them how lovely and shining their coat is, how soft too, how handsome they are. We sit at the window and talk about the weather a little when it's too wet or cold for a cat to enjoy going out, and we walk in the garden and talk about the sunshine or what trees are worth climbing when it's fine. Until recently we had a little black and white cat called Mono which liked to walk round smelling the flowers, and I used to talk to her about those and we'd try to decide together which were her favourites.

Kittens are much like young children— they benefit from cuddles and stroking. The early weeks and months can set the pattern for a lifetime, helping to determine whether they will be garrulous, people-loving adults or timid and highly strung

Sometimes it's necessary to speak reprovingly, in a sharper tone of voice which cats quickly learn to recognise as the one you use if you're displeased with something they've done or attempted to do, for example when they stalk birds (which ours do sometimes even though they know I hate it) or steal food (which they don't often but shouldn't *ever*). When training young cats to behave politely in the house, to get on reasonably well with their elders and with humans, they'll learn more quickly if you speak firmly, though still in quiet tones. *Never never* shout at them.

Cats can't talk back to us, but they certainly can make their attitudes clear. Now, as I write, I have a cat by my side which is eager to know what I'm up to and why I can't come out in the fields because it's a lovely day for a walk, all of which has been communicated to me in clearly understandable cat language by first coming into the room with tail up and a cheerful Prrp! greeting, then jumping impatiently on to my writing table, prrrpping rather querulously, then to the windowsill and looking out alertly, looking back at me and out again. On to my table again—much less clumsy and more silent than a dog would be, obviously, and no ill-mannered barking, but the message is the same—'Oh *do* come outdoors and have some fun!' So I had to explain that I'm writing, I must finish the day's allocated number of words, it's really for the good of us all. And now I have a quieter cat, resigned but under-

Left: Some cats are fascinated by mirrors and television, some hardly seem to notice they are in the room. Perhaps it's just a matter of temperament. Right: Then again, others just prefer a cat nap!

standing, sitting beside me and still longing to get me outdoors but indicating that patience is her greatest virtue . . . That was quite a conversation, that was!

Our cats have special tones of voice for different greetings—full and repeated Prrp prrps first thing in the morning when it's so good to be alive and you *must* get up and come out and what about breakfast? Single and a bit more casual as a quick Hello to a friend, passed often during the day on stairs or in a passage or in the garden, each intent on their own business. They have insistent noises when they want a door or a window opened and no one has noticed them sitting patiently willing it to open of its own accord; furious noises if no one comes or pays attention to earlier calls; seductive noises for when they want to beguile you; aggressive screams if they have to deal with an enemy; threatening growls if they want to intimidate an intruder; contented purrs for when life is treating them well (which I'm glad to say it almost always does). All this, of course, is the typical language of cats. But I'm sure that ours are more vocal, more liberated, more at ease in their self-expression because they live in a household where they are continually talked *to* as well as *about*, and are expected and encouraged to join in.

It's not really relevant, but talking of talking cats, have you heard the sad story of the single lady who lived in poverty with her doctored tomcat and dreamed wistfully of romance? Came the amazing day when her fairy godmother put in a belated appearance and offered her the traditional three wishes.

'Oh, I wish I was young and beautiful . . . I wish I was a princess, sitting on a golden throne . . . I wish my dear cat could be turned into a handsome prince!' No sooner said than done. What ecstasy!

But no. For then the prince who used to be the cat turned to his princess and said, with tears in his big green eyes: '*Now* aren't you sorry you took me to the vet?'

Oh dear!

Several years ago, someone in (I think) California claimed to have taught a cat to talk, actually to speak human speak. To prove it to the world at large, over the radio came a distorted but just about comprehensible voice proclaiming 'Ah love ma Mamma. Ah love

ma Mamma!' This was said to be, maybe was, that exceptionally intelligent and well-trained cat. I heard the broadcast and brooded over it for a day or two. I wasn't sure whether I believed in that talking cat or not, but at one point (I'm ashamed of it now!) I found myself thinking how marvellous it would be if Buffy or Maude could give voice to their affection in the same way. I looked at Buffy, who I know without being told loves me best of all (when she isn't thinking what a silly old woman I am, to be sure) and I said 'Do you love your Mamma, Buffy?' And she just looked at me, her great yellow eyes flashed with either scorn or amusement or both, and then very slowly she turned her back on me and sat down, her tail twitching slightly as it does when she wishes to convey extreme disapproval. Does Buffy love her Mamma? Yes, she does. But should I have asked her to say so? Not likely! A cat has her dignity and people who live with cats should have the sense to respect it. I love my Mamma, indeed!

Postscript: an American cat lover and expert on all things to do with cats, Anitra Frazier who is co-author of that excellent book *The Natural Cat*, believes that cats don't communicate with sound only but

'use the slow eye blink communication when they are feeling relaxed, contented and secure. I started practising whenever I could get a cat's attention and found that I received a return blink from the cat by the third try. Delighted . . . I began throwing these cat kisses to any and all cats with whom I came in eye contact . . . I was thrilled to discover that these strangers would automatically throw back a leisurely reply . . . Only twice have I had the experience of a cat doing a sort of double take . . . they seemed to be thinking "Hey, she speaks Cat!"'

And before you laugh, or say something sceptical and rude, I suggest you in turn find a cat, make eye contact and blow it a 'kiss'—just slowly but just for a second, just one blink and be careful not to screw up your face as you do it because according to Ms. Frazier that clouds the issue for the cat.

I've tried it and it works, really it does, every time!

Right: One of the most appealing faces . . . Who could resist giving its owner a special 'cat kiss' to show just how wonderful he is?

Astrocats

PISCES

As a friend of cats, and a firm believer that they are just as good (also just as bad, often) as humans, I don't see why we shouldn't share our interest in astrology with them and have horoscopes cast for our pets as well as for ourselves.

Well perhaps that's going a bit far. Think of the expense. If our Maude and Buffy were asked for their opinion they would no doubt suggest that the money would be better spent on salmon or fillet steak or other rare delights which cats are not usually asked to share, and leave the future to take care of itself.

But it's an interesting idea, and if you know the date and time of your cat's birth you can so easily find his/her birth sign. From then on it's up to you whether you look up his horoscope in the paper every day as you possibly do your own, and check what's in store for him, or whether you determine to take it more seriously, delve into planetary aspects and influences and learn how to interpret them for yourself.

Just for starters, you probably know that a horoscope cast by a professional astrologer is basically a map of the planets in the heavens at the exact time and place of the subject's birth. The map is in the

form of a circle, representing the path of the sun in the sky, and is divided into twelve signs of the Zodiac, or Sun signs. Your cat's Sun sign is determined just as yours is, by his time of birth: if he was born on or up to 30 days after the spring equinox on 21st March he will be an Aries, and so on through the eleven other signs—from April to May he would be Taurus, from May to June Gemini, from June to July Cancer, from July to August Leo, from August to September Virgo, from September to October Libra, from October to November Scorpio, from November to December Sagittarius, from December to January Capricorn, from January to February Aquarius and from February to March Pisces. To whet your interest, let's take a run through the signs and some of their qualities, and check up on your feline friend's astrocharacteristics.

Aries

Aries March 21–April 19. This is a fire sign, full of life and leaping energy. An Arian loves to be busy, to start something new (well it *is* the first sign of the Zodiac!). But he's also on the imperious side, sometimes inclined to act without sufficient thought, so your Arian cat could be a bit of a pickle— maybe in youth one of those kittens which get stuck up high trees and have to have the fire brigade come out to rescue them. My favourite astrology book tells me that Arians are highly competitive, they like to lead and to succeed; imagine the trouble a mother cat could have with a whole litter of them all wanting to come first all the time! A good quality: Arians don't believe in admitting defeat, will always go on trying whatever the odds, so if ever your Arian cat gets lost the betting is that he will somehow or other make his way home at last. A bad trait: they're inclined to start things and not finish them (catching a mouse, perhaps, and neglecting to dispose of it; digging a toilet hole and forgetting to fill it in).

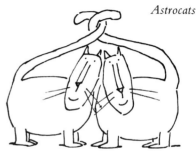

Taurus

Taurus April 20–May 20. An earth sign, ruled by planet Venus—sounds a bit heavy, and could be self-indulgent! Taureans can be possessive and masterful, fond of good living and material possessions, comfort-loving and determined. I see in my mind's eye a big fat tom cat, probably neutered, firmly installed in the most comfortable chair/cushion/bed/hearth rug in the house; happily well fed and absolutely in control of both his owners and his environment. Such cats sometimes stray if everything doesn't come up to standard—I know at least one which apparently became dissatisfied with life where it began for him (just down the road, as a matter of fact); he manifested himself one day on a neighbour's doorstep, cased the joint for a few moments taking in the warm fire, the cosy room, twitched his whiskers delicately in recognition of the delicious smell of stew coming from the kitchen, leapt firmly on to the best chair and has made it his own ever since in spite of constant pleas from his first people to come home. So do cosset your Taurean cat, if you want to keep him yours. Bad point: Taureans are capable of jealousy—he'll prefer to be the only pet around the house, won't want to share you with anyone. Good point: in return they're intensely loyal—he'll love you to distraction, pine if you go away, sit on your bed (provided it's soft enough!) and purr to you softly if ever you're ill.

Gemini

Gemini May 21–June 21. A light as air sign, ruled by Mercury; volatile and swift. Human Geminis are thinkers, talkers, writers, communicators; so a Gemini cat is likely to be very vocal—welcoming you effusively when you've been out of his sight for a few minutes, chatting to you, ordering you about, not mincing his words if you fail to produce supper on time or leave the door shut when he wants to go out. A Gemini cat will like to learn, whether just tricks such as playing with a clockwork mouse or cleverer things like the meaning of specific words and phrases you use when you talk to him. He isn't an idle cat, he needs to keep busy, so he'll do a lot of watching-out, coming-to-tell and so on. Geminis enjoy travel, so if you put a collar and lead on him he'll probably be happy to come for walks, may even relish a run in the car (remember to restrain him when the doors are opened or he could dash out and get lost). Difficult quality: Geminis aren't much attached to material comforts, or even to people, and they're inclined to be fickle—so he could grow tired of his home and set off to seek adventure. Saving grace: He's so charming, so intelligent—you'll remember him with affection even if he does decide to behave with such ingratitude.

Cancer

Cancer June 22–July 22. This is a water sign, ruled by the moon. Some say that people born under it, whether male or female physically, have a strong bias towards feminine interests and skills. Certainly most Cancerians are home-loving and have a deep need for security. Like their symbol, the Crab, they hide shyness and vulnerability underneath a seemingly hard outer shell. Most of the time they are frank and friendly, but because of the inconstant moon which rules them they are capable of becoming cold and remote. And how does all this tie in with your Cancerian cat's character? Well who's that sitting on your windowsill crying to the moon as long as her path of retreat is open behind her—when a braver soul would be out on the wall challenging all comers? Who's the disdainful lady who won't acknowledge your friends when they arrive to supper but decides to do the rounds for a purr and a stroke just when it suits her, after coffee? And Cancerians, it's said, are masters of passive resistance—but then so are all cats at one time or another. High point: if you have an unspayed female cat born under Cancer she should make a marvellous mother—conscientious, long-suffering, endlessly loving and patient. Cancerians are vain, so she'll fall into beautiful poses and be delighted when people praise her; Cancerians are tenacious, so be prepared for long battles when she decides to have her own way.

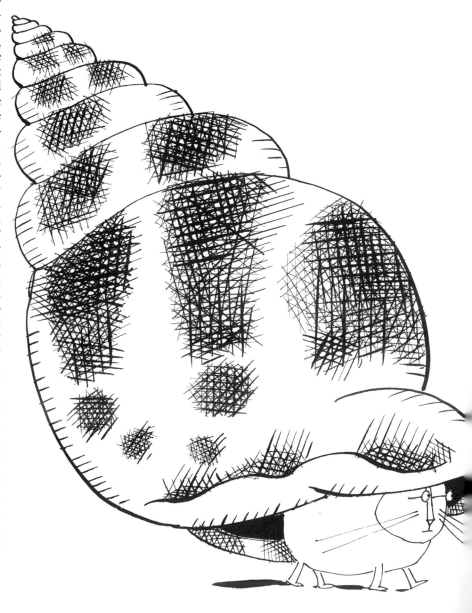

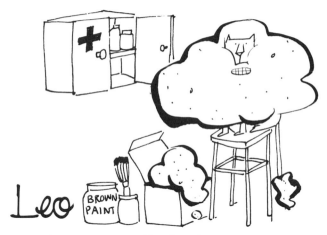

Leo

Leo July 23–August 22. Another fire sign, splendidly ruled by the sun, so a true Leo should be strong and noble, forceful and good, bringing light, inspiration and vitality to all who meet him. Leo people are often proud, often generous; they like to be the centre of attention. A Leo cat will revel in admiration and praise; he will love people to stroke him and tell him how handsome and beautiful he is. But at the same time he should have an easy-going, generous disposition: he won't rush in to supper and complain if another cat gets there first—why should he, after all, when he's perfectly confident that all is well in his splendid world and there's bound to be enough food for everybody? If, however, someone steals from him and he realises that he has been unfairly 'done down' (such as someone stole that juicy sprat he hid for a midnight feast), he will fight for his rights and almost always win because his sense of injustice makes him super-strong. Caution: Leos are *very* loving—if you can't face the thought of yours having a constant companion of the opposite sex, with kittens abounding, you should have him/her doctored early on in life or he'll be out on the tiles all night long.

Virgo

Virgo August 23–September 22. Born under an earth sign and ruled by Mercury, human Virgos are perfectionists—hard-working, precise, meticulous, critical, difficult to live with if you can't measure up to their high standards. I once had a friend who kept two cats in a London flat all week (luckily they spent weekends in the country so their lives weren't too closely circumscribed). They had of course to use a litter box when in London because there was no garden to scratch in. I didn't know that the older cat was a Virgo until I watched her one evening tidying up the box after her Gemini friend and before she could use it herself—scraping it, patting it, arranging it so that all was just so, then after her own penny was spent scratching and patting and tidying all over again until she'd left it as she would have liked to have found it. That was a Virgo, that was! Virgoans enjoy good food but are—yes, you've guessed it—finicky eaters; with a Virgo cat you must be more certain than ever that his plate is clean for every meal, and never too full, and that the milk or water in his drinking bowl is fresh every day. Possible drawback: on the whole, Virgoans are not very romantic—you may find your Virgo cat lacking in affection. Probable credit: if you can get him to concentrate his passion for work on catching mice—if there are any in your house of course—he won't rest until your whole property (and your neighbour's too!) is free from them.

Libra

Libra September 23–October 22. In keeping with their symbol, a set of scales, people born under the air sign of Libra, ruled by Venus, are even-tempered, even-handed, with a strong sense of justice. They are good at co-operation and compromise, they find fulfilment in love and marriage. If you are so lucky as to acquire a Libran cat, he or she is likely to make you a purrfect companion. He will be friendly and biddable, easy to train and easy to satisfy—all wholesome food will appeal to him, he will eat what is put on his plate without demur but will never be so greedy as to ask for more. Last thing at night he will stay out only for the prescribed ten or fifteen minutes, returning briskly the moment you open the door and call his name. He's less likely than the average cat to destroy furniture or carpets by sharpening his claws indoors; he won't scratch adults or even tiresome, teasing children; he won't sit on babies; he'll give up your chair nicely when you ask him to, even if he's only just curled up on it; he'll make a proud father and (if he's a she) a devoted mother. In fact he/she will be unlikely ever to put a paw wrong. Only drawback: could life with him turn out to be a tiny bit dull?

Scorpio

Scorpio October 23–November 22. A water sign this, ruled by both Mars and Pluto, tremendously powerful, energetic, resourceful. Some say that Scorpios are their own worst enemies because they feel and act so intensely, refuse to take life lightly, despise weakness, insist upon speaking out if they think they must, regardless of tact, timing or consequences. But their strength of feeling also gives them great staying power and resolution: if you sold your house and moved miles away, leaving your Scorpio cat behind with the new owners, you might easily find him on your own new doorstep a few weeks later, emaciated but determined (and furious with you into the bargain!), because he's the sort of chap who just will not be left behind, will not suffer injustice, will not give up. And if you didn't pick him up at once, apologise for your action but explain that you thought it was for his own good, praise him for his brave but foolhardy deed, he might just as easily turn straight round and go painfully back whence he came, having decided that you weren't worth making all that effort for after all! Scorpio cats, like Scorpio people, are more often than not strong and healthy; they have keen intuition, too—some seem to know more about their owners than said owners would like, anticipating their actions in the most uncanny way. They're sexy—watch out for undesirable followers. Beware: Scorpios will fight to the death if they think their cause is just. Rejoice: Scorpios are generous and compassionate in victory—he may even lick your poor hand where earlier he wickedly scratched it, if you care to let him that is!

Sagittarius

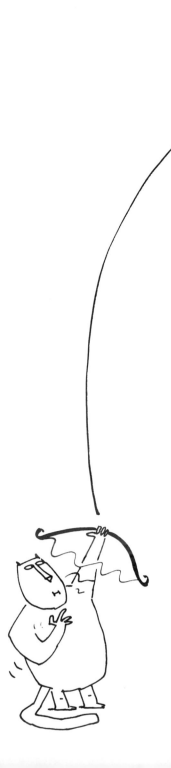

Sagittarius November 23–December 21. This is another fire sign, ruled by Jupiter and represented in the Zodiac by an archer. Sagittarians are energetic, hard-working, honest; their ruler, Jupiter, seems to protect them against many of life's ills and accidents. On the whole they're open-minded, just and kindly, though sometimes because they take a fairly simplistic view of life they may tend to become a bit set in their ways. They believe in plain speaking: have you ever been sworn at by a Sagittarian Siamese for producing supper an hour late? I have, and it's quite an experience. She looked at me, lashed her tail from side to side, then opened her mouth and said 'Yuck' or 'Aarggh' or whatever it was at top volume with pulverising force. The whole neighbourhood must have heard. There was no doubt whatsoever that I had failed in my responsibility, subjected a good cat to near starvation, and been an absolute failure as a cat minder. 'Yuck,' she repeated, fortissimo. But half an hour and a decent helping of pig's liver later she was so kind as to come without being asked and sit on my lap and say 'I forgive you now', having reverted to being a straightforwardly loving, practically purrfect Sagittarian cat again.

Capricorn

Capricorn December 22–January 20. Born under an earth sign, ruled by Saturn, symbolised by the mountain goat, Capricorns are sure-footed (try inviting a Capricorn cat into the bathroom and he'll immediately take a stroll round the edge of the tub, curiously gazing at your poor fur-less body and not troubling in the least to look where he's putting his paws). Capricorns are independent—every cat a Capricorn, then? —and self-sufficient; they like to look after themselves. A little Capricorn cat will honour his/her owner by accepting food and shelter, but with reservations: if he wanted, really wanted, he could always provide for himself somehow, that seems to be the message. Though on the other hand if you prefer to do it for him he's far too polite to deny you that pleasure. Part of his make-up, due to the heavy influence of Saturn, is melancholy: he will have black moods sometimes, you may even come upon him sitting thinking on an upstairs windowsill, brooding over the world below. If you dare to stroke him out of it you'll only get a hiss and a growl and maybe a scratch for your pains. Better to leave him alone then, until he feels happier.

Aquarius

Aquarius January 21–February 18. This is an air sign, ruler Uranus, symbolised by the water carrier. Aquarians believe in friendship, they love company and enjoy meeting new people. Although they can be opinionated, and get into arguments, these are soon settled because they don't bear malice. Reflected in cat terms, this means I think that a household full of Aquarian cats would get along very well: there might be the occasional spat but then sense would reassert itself— cats which quarrel among themselves upset the whole family, and what's the point of that. Aquarian cats like meeting new humans, that's for sure—they're outgoing and affectionate. Very unlikely to hide when visitors appear, they would much rather stay and be made a fuss of. Aquarian cats are great sitters on windowsills, they like looking out at nature from a position of comfort but are not as a rule great hunters. Watch out: they can be stubborn, so bear in mind that if he's told not to do something he may stop for the moment but will be determined to get his own way in the end! He may be of a rather nervous temperament, which is a worry; but intensely loyal and loving, so you should repay him by making his life as stress-free as possible.

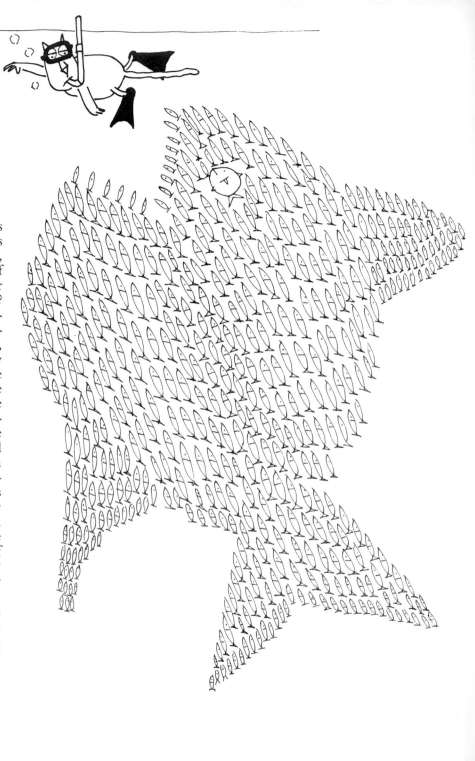

Pisces

Pisces February 19–March 20. This water sign, symbolised by two fishes swimming in different directions, seems so unsuitable for cats—yet of course there must be cats born under it, so what sort of cats are they? Pisceans are as a rule gentle and sensitive, and so are some cats (particularly the Longhairs, oddly enough, in spite of their frequently grumpy expressions). Your Piscean cat, like his human counterparts, may have difficulty in making decisions (those fishes are pulling both ways, remember); he will be most unlikely to be in any way combative and will allow other cats to dominate him rather than assert his rights to territory, food or even females. If things go well for him—and mostly they should, because he has great charm and is often much loved—the Piscean cat will enjoy his life. But if fate is unkind he won't resist, simply hide away and suffer. He'll appear to be a dreamy cat, self-centred too; but on occasions he'll surprise you with his intuition—some day when you're not feeling all that good, and sitting alone moping, he'll appear at your side or even jump on your knee, purring and saying 'Cheer up, cheer up, here I am. You've got at least one friend in the world— that's me, you know, and I'm here to help you, so cheer up cheer up! . . .' And you will, for how could you resist him?

O cats, have I done well?

Have I told all there is to be told about you—all, but still not too much?

Since cats have never found it necessary to learn to read, probably I shall never know the answer.

Though I might, come to think of it, read a chapter or two to Maude and Buffy as we sit beside the fire some winter evening, and see what they think. If I dare!

O cats, you are such infinitely superior animals.

But you are also our beloved companions, our dear familiars.

O cats, I salute you.

Bibliography

I am only an amateur cat minder, and make no claim that what I have to say about them is the ultimate wisdom. But our cats indicate to me (most of the time, at any rate) that I don't do too badly by them — which I hope is a good enough reason for passing on such knowledge as I've acquired. Much of it comes from personal experience, but on lots of occasions I couldn't have coped without researching expert opinion and knowledge, and I'd like to take this opportunity of saying thank you to all those whose books are listed below: they've been a source not only of information and help but of inspiration too. If you love cats, all of these deserve a permanent place in your home.

The Observer's Book of Cats, published by Warne's; *Champion Cats of the World*, published by Harrap; *Cat Lover's Diary*, published annually by Collins; *The Complete Cat Encyclopedia*, published by Heinemann; *The Long Haired Cats*, published by Batsford. All by Grace Pond, FZS.

A Standard Guide to Cat Breeds, published by Macmillan; General Editors Grace Pond, FZS and Doctor Ivor Raleigh. Consultant Editor Richard H. Gebhardt.

The Cat, An Owner's Maintenance Manual, by David Taylor, FRCVS. An Unwin paperback.

The Natural Cat, A Complete Guide for Caring Owners, by Norma Eckroate with Anita Frazier; Thorsons Publishers.

Sherley's Cat Book, 'The Complete Book of Cat Care', published by the Sherley's Division of Ashe Laboratories, Leatherhead, Surrey.

Cats, by Howard Loxton; A Kingfisher Guide published by Ward Lock.

The Wildcat, by Ernest Dudley; published by Frederick Muller in their series 'Our Unknown Wildlife'.

Animal Heroes, Military Mascots and Pets, by J. J. Kramer, published by Secker and Warburg.

The Animal's Who's Who, 1,146 Celebrated Animals in History, Popular Culture, Literature and Lore, by Ruthven Tremain, published by Routledge and Kegan Paul.

Index